AURA CHILD

AURA CHILD

The incredible story of a special gift

A I Kaymen

ISBN 978-1-907203-71-8

Typesetting by Wordzworth Ltd
www.wordzworth.com

Cover design by Titanium Design Ltd
www.titaniumdesign.co.uk

Printed by Lightning Source UK
www.lightningsource.com

Cover images by Nigel Peace
with thanks to HDResolutions
Photographs by Nigel Peace

Published by Local Legend
www.local-legend.co.uk

Dedicated to my parents, for all their love.

This is one of the most astonishing books you will ever read, the story of a very special child.

Everybody has a gift, but some are more special than others. And some are perhaps more of a curse than a blessing. Imagine growing up seeing the world in a completely different way to everyone you know, in a way that nobody – even your own family – can understand or will even acknowledge…

You see every person's energy field around them, and you watch how it changes as they speak, as they eat… you can even watch their thoughts. You walk down a busy London street, blink, and find yourself in the medieval farm that was once there – and you converse with the spirits of that time and place.

You can't tell anyone. They'll think you're mad. They already call you a freak. So how do you live with your special gift?

A I Kaymen was born and raised in Edgware, north London. She has degrees in Political Science and in Diplomacy, has travelled over three continents, and has worked in the public sector as a statistician and analyst. She is also an amateur athlete and an artist. This is her debut book, brilliantly imaginative and asking all of us some very searching questions.

Contents

Prologue

I know I am a baby. I stare in wonder at my pudgy, dimpled hands awkwardly grabbing the air in front of me. The warm sun beats down on them and the cotton sombrero on my head casts a circular shadow that follows me as I crawl towards my mother. I am frightened of its darkness but the faster I crawl, the faster it seems to move too. Whichever direction I go in and however fast, so the round shadow travels too.

My mother is sitting on a low wall bordering the rear of the garden. She's making a clicking sound with something she holds in her hand. I stop for a while to watch her and enjoy the pleasure of the cool lawn on my naked knees. She smiles and I continue my awkward journey towards her as she coos at me unintelligibly. The presence of my mother confuses me sometimes. She means love and safety, yet I know that she is not a celestial being.

I use the wall to heave myself up into a standing position, groaning a little with the concentration and immense effort of the action. My hands grip the brick to take some weight off my weak leg muscles. I'll have to relearn this concept of weight. Right now it's important to discover what my mother's doing before my knees buckle. She begins talking to me in a language I don't yet understand but I know the words are directed at me because of the lilting and gentle tone she adopts.

She snips a twig from a plant and I watch as the little bubble around it turns a dark red. The plant is angry. My mother gets up to tend to my crying sister but I continue to watch the plant. I can't heal it yet with this useless infant body, so I reach out to touch it, willing it to gain some comfort from my touch. The bubble immediately changes from red to a pale gold and lets out a blue streamer from its pruned stump, like a phantom limb. Strong hands suddenly pick me up and I am hoisted over my mother's shoulder. I decide that I really do not want to be here.

I have always felt like an island in the sea of humanity.

This earliest memory of my life on Earth is one I seem to have kept for good reason. It is the exact moment that I knew I was separate to other people, that I existed in harmony with nature rather than humans; the exact moment it hit me that I was mortal and subject to the limitations – physical, emotional and spiritual – that we all experience with each rebirth. It's a horrible realisation that you're again at the mercy of everyone and everything, knowing that you'll only be back in safety when you die - and that can only be earned by living and learning the lessons you chose for this life.

ONE

Canons Park

Every place on Earth has its own unique vibrational energy.

I hated the house from the moment I set foot in it. Perhaps it was the fear that comes with beginning a new life and leaving familiar territory, but as I ascended the stairs one by one, the queasiness in the pit of my belly grew stronger. The small corridor leading to my new bedroom seemed to open in front of me like a big yawn and I suddenly felt an irrational fear of being swallowed alive by it. I turned around to check that my mother was still there. She wasn't, but I could hear her yelling orders at Dad to move boxes more carefully.

Turning back towards the door, I gently pushed the handle down. The door creaked open outwards and didn't stop until it banged against the adjacent wall and stuck there. Silence followed and I stood at the entrance to the room wondering if that was a bad omen of things to come.

I sat on the floor amongst the neatly labelled boxes that had been left there, and looked up at the walls and ceiling. Although it was bright and sunny outside, the room seemed dingy somehow and bubbly reflections of light danced on the surfaces around me as if I were under water. The atmosphere was thick and I had the odd feeling that time had stopped. I listened and watched. The room was small and cubic. It gave the impression of being a place where someone could be forgotten or left to die. The pipes running through the walls made frustrated clanging noises and the gossamer curtains whispered as they danced on the draught coming from the windowsill. My room had a story to tell me but I was too afraid to listen.

Somebody died here, I thought to myself as I sat, anxious and shivering, too scared to formulate my thoughts into words for fear that they might unleash a terrible fate onto me.

Then the house suddenly came to life as Mum entered through the front door, setting down bags and yelling for anyone within earshot to put the kettle on. She had an abnormally loud voice, though it seemed strangely distant upstairs in my room. It didn't matter as long as she was somewhere in the house with me. I knew I was safe then.

Later that morning as I helped Dad reconstruct a bed, I asked, "Dad, do you like this house? Don't you find it creepy? What made you choose it?"

"Well, it's exactly the kind of property that your Mum and I were looking for... blast this goddamn thing... sorry, you didn't hear that... it's just what we were looking for - period features, run-down, a project we can really... Look, do you mind bunking with your sister tonight?" Dad always went off on a tangent. I waited a few moments for him to continue but he said nothing.

"But Dad, why didn't you ask us what we thought? This house doesn't even have a loo." I had begun to whine and knew that at this point he would either switch off or cut the conversation short. He had a selective attention span.

"Because we didn't think you'd be interested. We saw the property and had to put in an offer right away - and the loo's outside by

4

the kitchen door." Full stop. He was losing interest already.

"That's not a shed, Dad?" I asked incredulously.

"Nope. You'll have to take a loo roll from Mum before you go. Okay?"

"Okay," I sighed.

Taking a step back, I watched as he fiddled with the plastic packaging around the screws. From as far back as I could remember, Dad had been the one saving grace in a world otherwise full of weird people who never noticed the same things I did. Most importantly, he always warned me when Mum was in a bad mood or hid me behind the furniture when she was on the warpath. I studied him in detail: the pale skin, overgrown and greying hair, eyebrows that were so faint they were sometimes invisible and the look of intense concentration as he battled with the plastic bag. I often looked for traces of myself in him, since I knew from an early age that I didn't resemble my mother in the slightest. He was the only person who had a blue aura, unlike anything I'd ever seen yet somehow familiar. To me he signified home, although I wasn't quite sure what that meant yet. All I knew was that he and I were very alike - and unlike all the rest.

"Dad, am I adopted? I don't mind if I am."

"No, why do you keep asking? Don't listen to your sister. I was there when you were born and you're definitely ours. Do you want to be adopted?"

"No, that's okay, thanks."

Dad had set out all the component parts on the floor as a forensic scientist might lay out tools. He studied them for a moment, rubbed his chin and then picked out a small plank of wood and a screw.

"Actually, we bought you at the Pound Shop," he said, trying to turn it into a joke the way he usually did. I didn't always understand his jokes, but the blue that surrounded him became so soft and comforting that I would often pretend that I did just to bask in it.

"I thought the milkman delivered me one morning. That's what Mum said." I started to giggle and Dad followed suit.

My parents had chosen to move during the summer holidays so that their children could be bonded into slavery for six weeks. Free labour meant the money saved could be redirected towards the house. We spent the rest of the afternoon in comfortable silence, unpacking boxes and assembling furniture.

I watched Mum unpack the crockery and arrange it in the newly disinfected kitchen cupboards. Every movement was forced, without consideration. If the crockery had been eggs, every piece would have smashed. She slammed the doors shut and yanked them open again. Every so often she would mutter something under her breath in French.

If those were eggs, I thought, she would have smashed two dozen by now, that's 24 eggs. According to the recommended allowance we can eat a maximum of four per week. So my family would lose one week's allowance plus one person would lose a second week. That's probably me. I'm the runt of the litter who hates eggs.

My gaze drifted to the top of her auburn head where strange little bubbles were dancing about a hand span above her. Unlike ordinary bubbles, they didn't float upwards and burst. These bubbles bounced a little above her or stayed put, as though they were parts of a weird headdress attached to her by an invisible mesh. Sometimes a new one would burst out of her head, shoot up and come to a standstill.

They're angry thoughts. Mum is analysing something that has pissed her off. Those bubbles are what swear words look like.

She turned to face me suddenly with dark, angry eyes and a menacing frown. I moved further back behind the door frame until only my head and fingertips were showing. She was still lost in thought, so I smiled at her to diffuse her rage. It worked. She dropped her shoulders and smiled back, looking a bit embarrassed.

"Vaness… Genevieve." She always said Vanessa's name first as a reflex, even when my brother Marcus or Dad were standing in front of her. Dad had circumvented the problem by giving us all totally unrelated nicknames. The only problem with that was that it ruined our credibility in public.

Mum washed her hands and gave me a finger of shortbread. I hated shortbread. To avoid an argument I waited for her to turn away before slipping it into my pocket. I often pocketed food that I didn't want to eat. This brilliant idea regularly backfired on me when I forgot to remove the food before putting my clothes in the laundry basket.

Well, I've been around for nine years and my tastes haven't changed. They'll have to stop giving me food I dislike. It can't be that difficult.

Dad walked in, obviously searching for something. He was hungry. I could tell by his body language that he needed to eat something and fast.

"Here!" I said, fishing the shortbread out of my pocket and dusting it off.

"Thanks, Tiger." Unlike me, Dad ate anything, even if it came with pocket fluff.

"I gave that to you." Mum was raising only one eyebrow, which meant she was peeved again.

"I wanted to save it for Dad. Anyway, I've never been keen on shortbread."

With a sharp intake of breath, Mum continued with the crockery. A dart flew out of her head and smacked Dad in the stomach. It travelled so quickly that I didn't catch the colour. Dad's stomach began to make a churning sound and he reached for the indigestion tablets he kept by the biscuit jar.

"So don't eat what's been in people's pockets!" Mum snapped. Dad put his arms up as if to concede defeat, and left the kitchen.

"Why are you standing, staring at me like this?" she roared. The bubbles above her head had joined together to make up a dark, monstrous helmet.

"Come on, Tiger, let's go to B and Q," came Dad's command from the front door. I scampered out of the kitchen and accompanied him to his DIY heaven.

That night I lay on the floor of my sister's bedroom, unable to sleep, staring at the Artex ceiling. At nine years old I was acutely aware of how little my sister enjoyed my company and how she put up barriers whenever I approached her. As a baby I had watched the cloudiness around her grow thicker until I could no longer see through it, and then I would cry.

I watched her sleeping for a long time. Vanessa was the antithesis of me; at eleven she already liked make-up and designer clothes and spent far more than she 'earned' doing chores. Very pretty and popular, she could hold the attention of a crowd without effort. She was fascinating to me and I spent most of my early childhood following her like a tail.

My thoughts were rudely disturbed by a loud moo. Heart pounding, I leapt to my feet and silently scuttled downstairs to find a large cow standing in the hallway staring back at me. As I reached out to touch it, a man with heavy boots appeared.

"Here's the one that got away," he said to the cow, then to me: "Shouldn't you be in bed? Whose child are you? Look like a gypsy."

"Get lost!" I hissed defensively.

"Genevieve Kelly, how dare you speak to me like that! And look at me while I'm shouting at you."

I turned round to find Mum glaring at me, hands on hips. The slivers of light from the streetlamps outside penetrated the patterned glass of our front door and illuminated random parts of her face. They made the furrows on her forehead appear deeper than they actually were.

"Mum? I wasn't talking to you. It was him. That man."

"Which man? Was there a man here?" asked Dad picking up the 'phone. Mum trembled. She was enraged rather than scared.

"Yes, he had a cow with him."

Dad slowly put the 'phone back on the charger and looked over at Mum. She hadn't taken her eyes off me. Suddenly, they both looked pale and frightened.

"Go to bed," commanded Mum.

As I went upstairs I heard them whispering to each other and could just about make out what they were saying.

"It's happened again, hasn't it? We need to do something…"

"I think we need to take her to the doctor…"

"…before she gets older and it affects her life…."

"It isn't normal, for God's sake…"

I knew exactly what they were talking about. This had happened before when I was five years old. I'd burst into tears at our family Christmas dinner after seeing some emaciated, dirty children carrying heavy crates from one end of the room, through the wall and down the road. Every so often they were whacked by a bearded man with a stick and a pocket watch. Mum had been terribly embarrassed and tried to explain to everyone that I'd been feeling ill and must be delirious (I was fine, of course). Dad thought I'd fallen asleep and had a bad dream (though I'd been running around and chatting until it occurred).

"They think I'm not normal," I muttered to myself as I climbed back into the sleeping bag. "What's normal anyway?"

"You've ruined my beauty sleep…" Vanessa moaned.

The next morning was bright and I awoke to the sound of twittering birds. I could smell something burning and, assuming it was breakfast, decided that now was the perfect opportunity to test out the escape routes in our new house. I was just about to stick my leg out of the bedroom window when Vanessa pulled me back in by the seat of my pyjamas. The elastic in my knickers made a stinging twang as they hit my backside, putting me in a bad mood with her for the rest of the day. The air around me turned a smoky, dark red.

Why does she find it so difficult to think before she does anything? I thought angrily.

"Marcus is coming home for the weekend and you know what that means."

I'd stopped listening to her the moment I realised she was complaining. I was averse to any kind of moaning, whinging, whining and complaining. That tone of voice sent me flying into a contained rage which meant I found it difficult to see past the dark red clouds for hours. So, instead of allowing my blood to boil and anger to fester, I would simply stop listening. I watched as Vanessa's mouth moved and no sound came out. It was like watching a silent movie - all the drama was there but without the clichéd and smart-arsed dialogue. She was not very logical and the fractured nature of the energy around her reflected that. Whilst watching Vanessa become more and more animated, I realised how much of one's message could be communicated without words.

"Genevieeeeeve, are you listening to meee?"

"No," I said, and walked out of the room leaving her squealing. Downstairs, Dad was crouching on the living room floor with an extended tape measure in his hand.

"Hi Dad. Has Mum burned breakfast?" I asked.

"Morning, Tiger. No, she's not back from shopping yet," he answered, taking a pencil from behind his ear, scratching his neck with it and putting it back again.

"Thought I smelled something, that's all."

"Listen Tiger, about last night, you were dreaming or sleep walking, weren't you?" he suggested, looking like a hopeful child in a sweet shop.

"Yes," I sighed. I didn't want Dad to worry or be hurt. He was the only ally I had at home and the only family member I actually understood on an energetic level. It was best to keep him on-side and happy.

Marcus was due to arrive after breakfast and I wanted to make sure that I wasn't at home when he did. It was not that I hated Marcus, I just found him utterly repulsive. He was loud, used foul language for no reason whatsoever and was surrounded by a grey, smelly cloud that apparently only I could see. He offended my already established and delicate female sensibilities, and every time he hugged me a small part of his grey cloud would cling to me like thick cobwebs. The next day I would feel drained and invariably develop a cold. So I ate, washed and dressed at breakneck speed and had climbed over the garden fence before anyone could stop me.

About a half mile down the road was Canons Park, in which was an old walled garden. I loved being alone outdoors and liked to think of myself as an explorer. The trees often had bubbles around them that made me feel warm and safe. I could talk to birds and watch the wildlife without running the risk of being bullied by other children (as was often the case before we moved). As I approached the rear entrance of the park, I saw a man sitting on a bale of hay, eating what looked like a large pasty. It was the same man I'd seen in our house the night before. He was very dark-skinned, lean and blond, with heavy boots and a funny-looking overcoat. I couldn't tell if he was tanned or just dirty. He had pale blue eyes that were fixed upon me as he ate.

"I'm sorry I told you to get lost. You scared me with your cow, that's all. What's your name?"

"Matthew," he said, motioning for me to sit down next to him. Before I could react, he threw an apple that audibly bonked me on the forehead and fell into my lap. I wondered if my head was hollow. Matthew shook his head and laughed silently. I noticed he had some back teeth missing and a scar running from his ear to the corner of his mouth.

"Where did you get that?" I asked, pointing at the white streak on his face.

"One of the horses kicked me. They don't take well to being hoofed sometimes. Sorry about the cow, she must've wandered into the wrong field. I usually let them pasture by the old oak tree back there." He got up and stretched. I watched him walk away, feeling the thud of his heavy footsteps grow fainter.

"Can I see your horses one day?" I called after him.

"'Course you can," he called back, without turning around.

I could hear Mum calling me in the distance, tempting me back with fig rolls. *She must be close by,* I thought to myself. *I'd better get going.*

Mum was very efficient and didn't believe in superfluous gestures of affection such as hugging, kissing and using the words 'I love you' in any context. She communicated love to her children through home-cooked food, good clothes and keeping us tidy, and later by an avid interest in our academic studies once we were old enough to take care of ourselves. I preferred her this way because I never felt smothered, though Vanessa often resented her for it.

As I jumped back over the fence I caught the distinct scent of Marcus and groaned. My foot got caught and I landed on Dad's new sweet peas, bringing the trellis down with me. I groaned. Being in trouble twice in two days was not a good idea, especially when both parents were suffering from 'moving-home syndrome'. I resisted the idea of lying to them and just hoped that Dad wouldn't notice until the next day and that a freak storm would hit Edgware that night and take the blame for me.

"There's a good side to all situations – you just have to look for it", I muttered to myself, mimicking Dad's voice. "This might even work to my advantage. Mum will get angry, we'll fight and I'll be grounded or have an excuse to escape. I can bypass Marcus!" I picked the remaining bits of debris off my trousers and slunk in through the back door. Bizarrely, Mum was not back yet although Marcus was. He was leaning against the kitchen counter, sipping a cup of coffee. The greyish cloud surrounding him was darker today, and tinged with an odd yellowish green. I would learn later that this is what marijuana does to you.

Maybe I was imagining Mum's voice and just craving fig rolls, I thought.

"Hey, Gene," Marcus said, waving his hands half-heartedly.

I abhorred being called Gene. Every so often somebody would subject me to a tuneless rendition of *Singing In The Rain*, thinking themselves very smart and original as they did so. Irritation surfaced as I stood looking at Marcus; little spots of dark red were floating away from my belly, up to my throat and across to my brother. He smiled slightly and ran his hands through his overgrown mane of hair. Marcus was a good-looking male version of Mum, but it wasn't often I could see beyond his cloudiness and misery. We'd spent a lot of time together when I was little but I could only remember small snippets of that whereas I recalled every detail of my interactions with Vanessa. Only scent and sounds brought back memories of Marcus and I was indifferent to them. Before he went to university his room would reek of fags and smelly socks, so how he got away with being Mum's favourite was beyond comprehension. He was a slob and it was a miracle that he bathed every day.

Mum thundered in with several bags of shopping and a mini tree.

"Genevieve! I've got fig rolls for you! Genevieve…" she bellowed, as she turned round and realised I was only inches away

from her mouth. My ears popped. "Why are you standing there while I'm shouting for you? Oh, Marcus, my Marcus," she cooed, turning towards him. "Welcome home. Have you got laundry?"

Fig rolls were a sign that I was not in the doghouse after last night. Had Mum been angry, there would have been no mention of them and breakfast would have been Weetabix without chopped banana. We made a beeline to the kitchen where Mum quickly and efficiently put the groceries in their designated places and began to heat pans. I noted that Marcus did not offer to carry any of the shopping or the mini tree.

I loved observing people and mealtimes were good for that. My sister and brother were very alike in looks and mannerisms. They both licked their knives and had Mum's features, although Vanessa reminded me of Dad too when she smiled. They barely interacted with one another on any level other than the odd word, and I got the feeling that Marcus thought Vanessa was pointless. In fact I would watch the cloudiness around my brother become more compact when Vanessa was around, as though it were blocking her out. It never did that with me. On the contrary, it would try to surround me as though containing me in a kind of imaginary embrace and I'd become frightened. As I sat there waiting for everyone to finish eating, I again wondered why I didn't resemble either of my parents. The only thing I'd obviously inherited was Mum's sole bad feature, her hair. *Guaranteed to provide at least an hour of aggravation for any hairdresser. It has a life of its own and will not be tamed,* I thought, as my eyes followed the swirling mistiness around me.

"Stop staring at me, you little shit," said Marcus, a second before Dad clipped him round the head. After lunch I was able to avoid Marcus, which suited me fine, as he stayed downstairs talking to Mum about how broke and miserable he was. But then Dad discovered the trellis and all hell broke loose. Amid the ensuing pandemonium I was given strict instructions to stay out of sight so I obediently walked out of the front door and walked the mile and a half to Joe's house.

Joe had been my best friend since we both wet our pants during story time at Little Stanmore Nursery. He was fascinating to stare at. His skin, hair and eyes were all the same shade of mocha brown. Sometimes a wonderful orangey cloud, which was particularly clear and dense after he'd been playing football, would emanate from his limbs and chest. He made me happy and I would often stand near him just to absorb some of his energy.

He lived with his parents and brother in an ordinary semi with ivy growing over the front façade. Every year his brother would be hoisted up onto his dad's shoulders to cut the ivy away from the windows. It was a comical sight, a grown man barking orders to a tottering adolescent with clippers. I did ask why they didn't just hire a gardener. Joe's mum explained that after coming here penniless from India, her husband didn't see the point in spending money unnecessarily and put it in a college fund for the boys instead. She herself had been disowned for marrying a coloured man. Their garage was full of odd bits and scraps, as Joe's father spent his spare time inventing useless but fascinating things.

"Necessity is the mother of invention, kids," he would say, as he ushered us out of the garage and arranged his safety goggles.

As I arrived I could see that Joe was attempting to water their front garden, his skinny, endless limbs glistening with water. His clothes were wet too and he looked dishevelled, but to me he appeared as bright as a ray of sunshine. I guessed that he hadn't checked where the hose was pointing before switching the mains on. He looked so confused that I couldn't stifle the giggles that began to bubble up. Joe turned towards me, and I was drenched within seconds.

"Sorry! I wet myself too, see," he said, furiously pulling wet tendrils of hair away from my eyes. "I don't know how it happened." I had a theory about Joe's clumsiness: he was born on April Fool's Day and was jinxed from birth. We grinned at each other and I began to sneeze.

The land on which we walk is the only true constant in an ever-changing world. Never claim to own it.

I didn't see Matthew again until later that month. As per usual, I was wandering around the park touching the trees when I chanced upon his stables. He was grooming his horses so I chose not to disturb him. Instead I stood behind the stable door and watched him through a gap in the wood. From what I'd seen of him, Matthew looked ruthless and cold at the best of times, his steely eyes pierced straight through you and searched your soul without betraying any hint of emotion. He'd be a terrible person to make an enemy of. Had he admitted to murder, it would not have surprised me in the slightest. Today, however, I saw a different Matthew, tenderly running a brush down a horse's flank and following each stroke very gently with his other hand.

"Come out, whoever that is behind the door and speak to me, man to man!" he bellowed, as he turned on his heel to face the door. One of the horses bucked a little, startled at the sudden change in his voice. The others didn't seem to care, perfectly secure in his company.

"I would if I could, but I can't because I'm not a man," I said, as I tugged at the heavy door and stepped inside. "How did you know I was there?"

"Because you were blocking the light. I know every hole and space in my door. By the way, you're standing in a fresh one."

I looked down to find that my sandals had disappeared into a horse pat. Matthew strode towards the door, scooping me up on the way and flinging me over his shoulder. As I looked back, his horses were all staring at me and I could read jealousy on their faces. Matthew stood me on a tree stump as he pumped water onto my bare feet and then my sandals.

"When are you going to teach me to ride a horse?" I asked.

"When you're older and stronger. The horse wouldn't feel your weight enough right now. People make the mistake of thinking they can just jump on a horse and go. Then they complain when they fall off and break their bones. There's much to learn first. You have to bond with the horse so that you trust each other. Anyway, you're not tall enough either."

He wiped the top of my feet with his shirtsleeve and handed me back my sandals. I struggled to keep up with him as he walked back to the stable, my every footstep squelching noisily.

"Where are you from, Matthew?"

"Near Bristol. Any more questions? I hate talking – it's a waste of my time," he snapped.

"Do you have any children?"

He stopped working and looked down at me. It was an intense look but not angry, almost as if he were subconsciously debating something. He put on a coat and walked outside again, beckoning for me to follow. After what seemed like an hour, but was really only ten minutes, he stopped. In front of us was a row of three tiny gravestones sticking out of the long grass.

"There are my children," he nodded at the gravestones. "My sons. Not one saw his first birthday. All came too early and went too early." He folded his arms and looked at the graves for a long time. There was not a trace of emotion on his face. Even so, he looked like the loneliest man on Earth at that moment.

"Didn't you have a girl then?" I asked gently.

"No, wouldn't have any use for one, either. Girls can't work on the land like men can."

"Your wife's a girl, isn't she?"

"Aye, she's a good woman," he said, turning towards me and squatting down so that our eyes were level. "I've never showed this to anyone, so don't mention it again." Matthew turned and started walking back to his horses. Every now and again he would look back over his shoulder.

I was in trouble when I got back home, and this time Dad was the angry one.

"Where the hell have you been, young lady?" he asked sternly.

"In the park, talking to … trees." I realised how daft it sounded but I couldn't risk another 'cow' episode.

"What? Mum was worried when you didn't turn up for lunch. I thought you were tidying your room. How the hell did you escape? Bloody Houdini!"

I had no idea what a houdini was but made a mental note to ask Joe later. Joe had a whole set of encyclopaedias and therefore had access to endless information on a wide range of topics. Dad was still telling me off but I'd stopped listening ages ago. My attention had turned to a mysterious whipping sound that had started up outside and was hypnotising me with its rhythmic regularity.

Dad eventually gave up and let me go, shaking his head and muttering to himself, so I made my way to the living room where Mum and Vanessa were watching television. Their choice of programme didn't interest me in the slightest; I'd been drawn to the room by the whipping sound – it was a little louder here, although no less mysterious. It must have been about twenty minutes or so before I glanced across the room to see that Mum wasn't watching the television. Instead, she was watching me with a certain look on her face. I looked back, trying to fathom what was behind the mask; it was neither pity nor regret nor sorrow but it had faint traces of all three. It was as though she was struggling to understand me. There was a grey smokiness emanating from her heart that seemed heavy and sticky like snot. Every time she sighed it would wobble. This is how I would remember my mother.

As I looked back at her I realised that this was why she treated me differently to the others. There would be times when she gave me an extra serving of food or took care to wash my hair very gently, as if afraid I would break. Yes, she did sometimes favour me over a perpetually hungry Marcus and a screaming Vanessa; I was never made a victim of her brutal efficiency the way they were.

Vanessa stirred. It was a commercial break.

"You're a weirdo," she said, as she walked past me and noticed that I was crouching in the corner with one ear pressed to the wall.

Later that evening Joe came over. It was the perfect opportunity to test my hearing.

"Do you hear it, Joe?" I whispered, as Mum ladled out onion soup. She gave me an extra ladle full.

"Hear what?" he asked aloud. Sometimes Joe was a bit slow on the uptake.

"Hear what?" asked Mum, a little too sternly for comfort. I squirmed a little before composing myself.

"Oh nothing. I think I might have tinnitus is all," I replied, as nonchalantly as I could. Everybody looked at me in stunned silence.

"How do you know what that is?" asked Mum. I didn't have a clue how I came to know. I just did. Sometimes words and ideas would just enter my head as though they'd been whispered to me.

"Told you she was a weirdo," muttered Vanessa, as she slurped her soup from the bowl.

Being a silent observer was what I looked forward to most at mealtimes, rather than the actual food. There was something about the way a person treated their food that spoke volumes about their true personality. After an initial flash of annoyance that clouded my vision, I relaxed and watched Vanessa eat. However elegant she was to look at, she had no sense of etiquette at all. Lately I'd begun to notice how little she actually enjoyed her food, as her energy became duller and denser at the mention of it, like a barricade. There was no sense of happiness around her when food was put in front of her. Instead, I got the distinct feeling that Vanessa thought it a chore to eat.

On the other hand, I loved watching Joe. He relished his food and sometimes didn't even bother to chew it before gulping it down. Unlike me, he would dive into whatever was on his plate and mix everything up first. He enjoyed creating a kaleidoscope of colours and flavours even before putting the first spoonful into his mouth. The oddity of his table manners was very similar to the swirling that took place around his torso when he started to digest his food. It looked like a desert sandstorm I'd once seen on television. I was convinced that Joe's lack of chewing was very closely related to his lack of caution. He often didn't think before plunging head first into an action, and then wondered what on Earth he had got himself into. In this case it was indigestion – he spent the half-hour after dinner belching non-stop.

My indigestion is so different, I thought to myself. *It doesn't move so much. It's boring compared to his. I wonder why.*

I could not contemplate eating something that wasn't pleasant smelling or neatly arranged. I would spend hours chewing my food slowly and deliberately and was always the last person to leave the table. Joe didn't understand why but he kept me company long after his plate had been cleared away. The reality was that I was often trying to observe what effect my food was having around my body, which could take hours. I sometimes suffered stomach aches that the GP put down to an irritable bowel or attention-seeking behaviour. Mum insisted they were due to a weak constitution, inherited from Dad's side of the family. But I was convinced they were due to eating food that was aesthetically offensive. I learned later how wrong we all were – it was merely due to my being unable to stomach life.

My obsession with the aesthetics of food was down to my older brother and I secretly blamed him for not letting me enjoy food as a child. He would chew loudly, turning his food into a lumpy sludge, and when everybody else had turned away he would open his mouth at me. Marcus was disgusting. At other times he would bend down until his face was hovering only centimetres above his plate and, with the aid of a spoon, shovel and vacuum up everything in one sitting. On occasion his hair would flop forwards into his food too, and Dad would threaten to make him wear Vanessa's hairclips at the table. What was really unfair was that food did nothing to the cloudiness around him, and he never suffered from any form of indigestion.

I looked down at my soup. It was brown and that was not a good sign. We had crusty bread too so I ran the risk of getting crumbs in my soup that would eventually go soggy. There was also the decision of whether to put butter on my bread. Once I put butter on my bread I would have to rule out dipping it in my soup, as it would create tiny pools of fat on the surface. (I often wondered if that was the elbow grease Mum was talking about as she worked.) Joe sensed my dilemma.

"Tear the soft part out of the middle and dip that in the soup. Then eat the soup. Then eat the crust with butter. Good idea, right?"

I smiled at his ingenuity as he passed me some bread, but then froze as a group of faceless children ran across the dining room and into the garden through the closed back door.

The next few weeks passed by without me getting into trouble once. Marcus slept all day and socialised all night and Vanessa was busy with her latest obsession, tap-dancing. Joe came over daily to help me arrange my room and we spent most afternoons helping one of my new neighbours plant his rock garden and walk his overweight dog.

On the last Saturday of the summer holidays we held our house-warming barbeque. Mum was a little embarrassed that we still had an outdoor loo, but gained some comfort from the fact that she'd made it hospital clean and that many of her friends liked quirky period features. I sat by the fence with Joe stroking Buster, the fattest dog in Edgware, observing everyone. Buster had enveloped both of us in a big pink cloud that grew denser every time I stroked him. It was very difficult for me to move away from the comfort of Buster's pink cloud, so I sat where I was and simply watched everyone.

Among our many guests was Ravi, Joe's older brother. I was still too young to appreciate how handsome he was, but all the pubescent and adult females cooed over him and offered him titbits of chicken wings, prawns and ice cream. He had a rather spectacular effect on Vanessa too. The moment she noticed him, she gave off strong flashes of bright red and pink colour, and funny little streamers emerged from her heart and groped towards him. Seemingly oblivious to them, he covered his chest with folded arms and the streamers forlornly drooped before snapping back into Vanessa's chest. At this, she got upset and ran back into the house.

Early on Sunday morning, I woke to that sound of whipping. Cautiously walking downstairs, I mulled over the fact that it could be anyone or anything so, regardless of my large father and bad-tempered mother sleeping upstairs, it would be a good idea to protect myself. I giggled at the thought that it would be Mum who would cause more damage to any intruder than my passive Dad. I grabbed the air freshener from the telephone seat and gingerly tiptoed towards the back door. I needn't have bothered with the spray. On the other side of the door was a little boy. He couldn't have been more than five or six. He was skipping like clockwork and hadn't noticed me watching him through the back door glass. He was a beautiful child with butter-coloured hair and a perfect porcelain complexion. His flushed cheeks looked like drops of strawberry sauce slowly spreading through milk. I opened the door and he stopped skipping.

"Hello," he panted, "what's your name?"

"Genevieve. What's yours?"

"John Graham Davis," he announced proudly.

I looked around a back garden that somehow seemed different now: the fruit trees around the edge had been replaced by rose bushes, there were several pieces of bamboo garden furniture to one side, and a tree in the centre. The paved area with our barbeque had disappeared. I perched on the nearest bamboo chair and looked at John Graham. He smiled at me and sat on the chair opposite, tucking his hands under his knees and swinging his dangling legs.

"Are we friends now?" asked John Graham eagerly.

"Of course we are. Why would you think otherwise?"

"You speak like a grown up!" he giggled. "If Guineviere is your Christian name…"

"Genevieve," I interrupted.

"…sorry, I just finished reading about King Arthur. It was very interesting. What's your family name?"

"Kelly. Dad's Irish," I explained.

"My father's Irish too!" he squealed with delight. "But he was in India before I was born, with mother. We have lots of furniture pieces and souvenirs from there. Would you like to take a look? I'm so happy I have a real friend. I don't have any of my own." John Graham sighed and then smiled again.

My ears pricked up when I heard my mother's voice from within the house. I could tell by the tone of her voice and her heavy footsteps that she was annoyed with me.

"Where in God's grace is Genevieve now?"

"Not again," came Dad's muffled reply.

"I'd better go," I said. "But I'll see you later." I turned round to find that the bamboo chairs, the roses, the tree and John Graham Davis had all disappeared.

TWO

Walls, Floors and Ceilings

Maybe she knows that a loud voice will
cause my skull to shatter.

School started again the following Tuesday. Joe and I always tried to get there as early as allowed and get a desk towards the back or side of the classroom. We had an understanding that whoever got there first had to save the adjacent seat for the other. I ran down the road at full speed, decelerating only slightly when I dodged other children. School was a 1930s red brick box with a concrete playground and a strip of sports field behind it. It would have been a good contender for the Most Boring Building in Britain Award. The interior was just as bad, with sea-coloured walls and speckled grey floors. The notice and display boards were currently vacant so corridors and classrooms were completely devoid of any kind of character. In brief, it all added to the depression that most pupils were feeling that morning.

I found my coat peg and hung up my PE kit and coat before gingerly stepping over the threshold of the classroom. Joe was sitting at the front of the classroom, head down, arms folded tightly. He was annoyed about something. He looked up at me, his mouth so contorted with intense irritation that I could barely see the rest of his face.

"They've decided for us", he spat out in disgust.

"Relax Joe, I'll just swap labels with, er... Sun Chi. She doesn't like you after you spat a cherry pip at her last year so I reckon she won't mind."

I peeled Sun Chi's label off the desk with great care and swapped it with mine, a few seats away, then let Joe sulk while our classmates came in. Most faces were familiar, others not so, but everybody had the same expression of depression with a tinge of anxiety.

Mrs Harmon, our new class teacher, ushered in the few stragglers loitering by the door. She was a tired-looking, nondescript young woman in her mid-twenties. Her choice of clothing only made her look worse, the drab blue and grey tones washing out any life in her complexion and accentuating the circles under her eyes.

"Will you please take your seats?" she shouted, arms flailing, trying to contain the din of twittering children. "Good morning class, my name is Mrs Harmon," she then said through a forced smile.

"Good morning, Mrs Harmon!" we all chorused miserably. A short silence followed when we realised en masse that this would be our morning mantra for the next god-knows-how-many days until the end of the academic year.

Joe and I soon discovered that sitting at the front of the class had its advantages. We were often overlooked when Mrs Harmon picked on pupils to read aloud to the class, answer questions or be plant-watering monitor for the day. In fact, be the end of the first week most of us had warmed to Mrs Harmon. It was a pleasant surprise to discover that she had a sense of humour and had perfected the balance between being easy-going and disciplining us. Her throat would sometimes give off the most beautiful blue colour I had ever seen and it was obvious that she genuinely liked being with us. The only thing that we didn't like about her was her insistence that every child hold hands with a member of the opposite sex on the way to Assembly each morning. She explained that it was a good way for us to make friends and for her to ensure that we all got to the hall. As we marched down the corridor like a multi-headed caterpillar she would count us, two by two, like our very own female Noah. Joe balked at the idea and often spent Assembly grumbling and wiping his hand against his trouser leg. Sometimes he did the opposite of what Mrs Harmon told us and his stomach gave off a dirty red cloudiness that smelled funny. What I didn't realise at the time was that it was the start of a behaviour pattern that would eventually destroy him.

Falling back into the school routine was easy enough but getting used to being picked on by Philip and Daniella Blue was next to impossible. They had bullied me since kindergarten when they'd first noticed my lack of strength and stature. Philip would put spiders in my hair to make me cry and Daniella stole my bottle of milk on a daily basis (although that actually suited me fine as milk gave me wind).

I stood rooted to the spot, confronted by them as I left the toilets just outside the playground boundary. They were not identical twins but looked incredibly similar. They both had the same mousy brown hair, pug features and were as wide as they were tall. I couldn't bear to look at them sometimes as they gave the impression of not having washed. Neither of them ever had any definite energy pattern or colour around them and I assumed this was due to them being filthy or stupid. Later I would learn that it was just due a lack of self-esteem, which was also why they were bullies. Philip looked at me with piggy eyes and asked nastily:

"I saw your mum yesterday. Is she your real mum? I'll bet she's not. You're supposed to look like your family but you don't. You're ugly and gross."

"What would you know about genetics?" I retorted as sarcastically as a nine-year old could. To my annoyance, a band of thick air constricted my throat and my voice sounded like a squeak. I should have guessed that Philip wouldn't understand and instead of an answer he whacked me across the head with his fist.

"Try and give me brain damage but I'll never be as thick as either of you!" I hissed through clenched teeth. The pain began to grip me and out of the corner of my eye I saw Philip's fist swing back to hit me again. But then his arm dropped and both of them turned and walked away. I felt a warm hand clasp mine and pull me in the direction of the Welfare Office. I couldn't see clearly but I could tell it was Joe.

The Blues didn't bother me again for many days after that. They were terrified of what Joe would do in retaliation, being taller, sportier and far more foul-tempered than either of them. Philip had attracted his wrath on several occasions since nursery school. We would all be turning ten this year but it was already clear that Joe had the athletic potential to make something of himself and was respected by older members of the sports teams. Philip was secretly jealous but didn't have the audacity to make an enemy of Joe, knowing very well that he himself had no talent to fall back on or identify himself with.

Sure enough, a few days later, the Blues and two of their gang made the mistake of sitting in the classroom at lunchtime without the protection of a teacher. Philip was leaning back in his chair against a desk when Joe strode in, kicked the chair out from under him and, after watching him bang his head against the desk behind, strode out exactly as he had come in. I heard it on the grapevine later. Neither Philip nor Daniella made eye contact with Joe and me for the rest of that half term.

Around the first week of November, my life suddenly took a turn for the worse. That was when the nightmares started. I was swept up in a living hell with no way of escape. They came often, not differentiating between periods of stress or contentment, and followed a similar pattern. As I fell asleep, I would feel myself moving forward at great speed, the momentum almost too much to bear and terrifying me to the core. I would try to struggle and scream before realising that my body and brain had somehow become disconnected, and I was at the mercy of something unknown and threatening.

Once the sensation of rushing had passed, I would feel calmer and begin to float, higher and higher through the ceiling, the roof and towards the stars. Sometimes I would travel to other places - places with wars, strange places where people would float with me, or familiar places where I observed people I knew. Then the rushing and zooming sensation would begin again, but this time I would be sucked downwards, falling from the sky through the roof and ceiling and back into my sleeping body. I jerked awake, palpitating and hot, as if I'd just run a marathon.

By the age of ten I became a willing insomniac. I would do any-thing to avoid the curse of sleep, absolutely anything.

In the first autumn spent in that house, I enjoyed decorating my bedroom and really making it my own space. I had never had my own territory before, having shared with Vanessa all my life, and the peace of mind that came with privacy was wonderful. Vanessa had always created a line of socks to split our old room in half but the sense of territory never occurred to me as I was too young. I just thought she was being foolish.

This new independence gave me the impetus to branch out and earn my own pocket money too, a form of self-expression that I'd never tried before and it gave me a real sense of freedom. I started my own business, getting all the newspaper delivery rounds in the area and contracting them out to local children at a slightly reduced rate. That way, I made almost £10 a week doing nothing except collecting the papers and the money and chaperoning the smallest children to ensure they were safe. Most of the money was deposited in my savings account but I allowed myself a fund to buy nick-knacks, pictures and other necessities for my room. I hated posters (they were tacky) and framed pictures cost proper money. Already I had the nagging feeling that I should never allow myself to become financially dependent on anybody else, though I wouldn't find out why until much later.

Every first Saturday of the month, Joe and I would race to the local newsagents so I could buy us collectable stickers with the money I'd set aside for treats. However, the first Saturday in November was different. The cold I'd had for the previous week turned into a fever that enveloped me in a mist of delirium for two days and a night. In the midst of that delirium came five minutes of complete lucidity. I opened my eyes and gazed at the open bedroom door, waiting for somebody, anybody, to come in and put me out of my misery, when in burst two boys, wrestling and falling over each other like puppies. At first I thought they were playing but in fact they were fighting. They were older and fairer than Joe and Ravi, and one of them was chubby. As he scrambled to his feet, the older one looked at me, or rather at the wall behind me. He had the most attractive eyes I had ever seen, pale hazel with thick eyelashes. I tried to reach out but my arm would not respond. The other boy rugby-tackled him and they fell through the carpet.

"Come back! I'm bored!" I croaked.

Towards Christmas, school became a lot more exciting. There was the nativity play to rehearse for, the class Christmas lunch to volunteer for and the parents' evening to dread or look forward to, depending on how you looked at it. I sat at my desk one cold Thursday morning, carefully drawing a border around an eleven-page essay entitled 'A Short Story'. It been completed and edited to my satisfaction and all that stood between me and multiple house point glory were the last few finishing touches.

"What are you drawing?" asked a little girl standing to my left. I looked at her in astonishment, wondering how she managed to get past Mrs Harmon and invade the classroom. She had wavy, bobbed hair that was pinned back with a simple clip. Her uniform was somehow different although I wasn't sure how exactly, and she wore mid-length socks with sensible t-bar shoes that made her look old from the knee down. There were other children wearing equally sensible, old-fashioned attire standing behind her.

"We're playing tag. Come and play with us," she beckoned, running away from me. Tempted, I got up and ran after them, giggling at the prospect of making new friends.

CRACK! My forehead bounced off the classroom wall and I fell back, smacking the back of my head on the cold floor.

"Genevieve! What are you doing?" yelled Mrs Harmon. Her face appeared spinning and swirling before me, a horrified expression on it, and then everything went black.

I woke up feeling as though a slab of concrete had been left on my head. The pain was so intense that I let out a gasp as I slowly opened one eye.

"Genevieve, are you with me?" I recognised Mum's voice. She sounded gentler than usual. *Maybe she knows that a loud voice will cause my skull to shatter.* I groaned in reply. The pain was turning to nausea and forming words could result in vomiting if I wasn't careful. When I moved my eyes to look at her, the whole room seemed to follow.

"What happened? Your teacher said you just got up and ran into the wall. I told her that it's not something any sane person would do, let alone any child of mine. Did someone dare you to do it? Were you tripped up or pushed?" Mum sighed and squeezed my hand, holding my fingers in her warm grip. "I'll ask your father to speak to you. You'd feel more comfortable talking to him, you always do."

I groaned again. I wanted to tell her to give me a bucket but I was helpless. If I opened my mouth I would vomit, and if I vomited I would have to move which would hurt my head. For the first time in weeks I prayed for sleep and closed my eyes as Mum's voice faded into the background and the monotonous drone of the fluorescent lights took over. The drone seemed to be perfectly synchronised with the throbbing in my swollen head, filling my skull and giving me an alien sense of comfort as I drifted off.

Next morning I woke up to the feeling of bright sunlight on my eyelids. There was a nurse in the room, humming the chorus of Kylie Minogue's I Should Be So Lucky over and over to herself. She held a clipboard in her armpit as she vigorously wound the cord of the blinds around a hook on the wall. I watched as the figure of eight got fatter and fatter until there was no cord left. The nurse turned to me and smiled.

"How are we this morning?" she enquired brightly, her enthusiasm beginning to make me feel sick again.

"Why do I feel sick?" The words sounded hollow, feeble and distant and I wondered if I'd damaged my ears too.

"You have concussion, dear," she replied without the grin fading even slightly. "Here's something that will make you smile, dear - your dad is downstairs having some breakfast. He'll be up shortly. Daddy's girl, are we?"

It was something I had never thought about before, usually too busy trying to stay out of trouble. Contemplating it now made my head ache so I chose to look out of the window instead. The morning was beautiful and crisp, the glorious sunshine making an irony of the people outside who were bundled up against the chill. Just then, I detected some movement out of the corner of my eye and the wall by the window began to change, almost melting in front of me. To my horror, a face oozed out of it, a young serious looking man with thin-rimmed spectacles and greased hair combed into a side parting. The teeth of the comb had made neat, glossy rows.

"I say, can you kindly direct me to Obstetrics?" he asked in a startlingly deep voice.

I didn't dare move so he eventually gave up and melted back again; I continued to stare at the wall for a very long time afterwards, too frightened to scream and too nauseated to move. Rescue came in the form of Dad. He seemed his usual jovial self, with no hint of undue concern on his face or in his body language. Dad never showed any feelings of anger, worry or other negative emotions in front of us. He felt it was unnecessary. Sometimes that was annoying because the contradictory colours and patterns of the energy around him would confuse me. He was carrying a small tray of goodies, which he placed on my lap before plonking himself on a rickety plastic chair. On the tray were his coffee, a hot chocolate for me and several lopsided cupcakes topped with chocolate spread.

"Morning, Tiger. Believe it or not, Vanessa made those."

He pointed to the cakes and pulled a face. I couldn't help giggling. Vanessa hated to put effort into anything that involved getting her hands dirty and I guessed that Mum had made her do the washing up too. Dad's chair began to make an odd straining sound so he got up and sat on the empty bed next to mine.

"Seriously though, how are you feeling now? Is there anything you'd like to talk about? We kept you in that school because it would be more secure for you during the move, but if you're being bullied, Genevieve, then you can…." He trailed off as I closed my eyes.

"Can I come home?" I whimpered, desperately fighting back tears that had sprung up from nowhere.

"It's alright, love," Dad said, getting up and sitting next to me on my bed. I put my head on his diaphragm and closed my eyes again. "I'm bringing Joe to see you after school. You'll feel much better then." Dad's stomach vibrated with his words and my nausea miraculously disappeared as a new sense of calm washed over me. When I looked up, he was examining one of Vanessa's cupcakes as if it was a shelf bracket. "Want one?" Dad raised his eyebrows. "You slept through breakfast. We didn't want to wake you. The nurse said you needed sleep, see."

Vanessa's cakes were a pleasant surprise for her first attempt. I scraped the spread off mine as it interfered with the taste of the hot chocolate; I had once heard Mum exclaim that chocolate cake was the best remedy for a particular type of female ailment and I'd kept that in mind ever since, although I couldn't remember what the ailment was.

"Did Vanessa make anything else?" I enquired innocently.

"She had to," Dad replied between mouthfuls. "After using every utensil in the house to make these, Mum made sure she got as much use out of her in the kitchen as she could. She's made some fruit loaf with Mum's help and a chocolate brownie that was meant to be a sponge but collapsed. She's also booked to peel spuds for Sunday lunch so you're off the hook. Poor thing, she's been complaining about aching arms and slavery ever since."

I awoke later that afternoon when the nurse came back to take my blood pressure and help me to the toilet.

"Your Dad has gone to pick up your boyfriend and bring you some food," she explained, as she deftly washed my face and changed my robe. My cheeks were burning. Joe was *not* my boyfriend. "Would you like me to bring you something from the canteen? We have spaghetti Bolognese or vegetable pie and there's trifle for pudding."

"No thanks, I'm very fussy," I explained, not wishing to hold a conversation with her after calling Joe my boyfriend. Also, I couldn't bear the thought of a hospital lunch and my head had begun to throb again. "Can I have some fruit instead?"

"Sure, I'll bring you up a banana or something," she promised as she rolled her eyes.

"Did anything spooky ever happen here? Did anyone die?" I asked suddenly. I wanted to know about the man with glasses or whether I'd been hallucinating.

"Sweetie, this is a hospital," she said, adopting the tone of an adult speaking to a very young and stupid child. "People die here sometimes." She cocked her head to one side and looked at me. There was a brief pause. "You really have an overactive imagination, don't you? I'll ask Ruthie. She's been working at this hospital for over thirty years. She'll know a few ghost stories about this place."

Ten minutes later a matronly Afro-Caribbean woman in a bright blue trouser suit breezed in, much lighter on her feet than her large frame would suggest. She wore huge, chunky earrings and a silver crucifix around her neck. I hated costume jewellery, it was too gaudy and fake for my liking, but this lady made it look sophisticated and tasteful. She could have worn a bin bag and the sheer force of her character would have created the illusion of a designer dress. Joe was right about it never being about what you wear but how you wear it. The blue lady pulled up a chair and sat down so heavily that I could hear her thighs slap as they hit the seat. She had two bowls with her, one of which was carefully placed in my lap, full of something lumpy and white. Upon closer inspection I recognised the contents as fruit salad topped with cream. I smiled at the lady and a sigh of relief escaped my lips.

"Why the sigh, young lady?" she asked. Her voice was deep and throaty. The image of thick, flowing caramel ran through my mind with every spoken word as I listened. I loved her voice instantly.

"I thought it was rice pudding for a moment, that's why." As an afterthought, "I love your voice."

"Well, that's good, Genevieve Kelly, because I've come here to tell you a ghost story." She must have noticed my eyes light up as she took a scoop of her fruit salad and munched it with the excitement of a child eating cookies.

"Are you Ruthie?" I asked quietly.

"The one and only. I've been a receptionist for nearly thirty years and I could tell you some funny happenings that go on around here. But first you eat up and I'll tell you the story of Dr Waring before my break ends. Well, Dr Waring died way back in nineteen sixty, about a year after I started here. In those days not many people spoke to me unless they had to. Race relations!" she chuckled and her whole body bounced up and down. "Dr Waring spoke to me though. He was a nice young man. He kept bees as a hobby and often gave me fresh honey for my husband. He's got a sweet tooth but no longer got many teeth!"

She laughed again, her voice resonating up from her diaphragm and touching everything in the room with vibes of pure joy. "Anyway, there was something about Dr Waring that some folk didn't like. Apparently – I don't know for sure – he batted for the wrong side, if you know what I mean." She winked. I had no idea what she meant but I didn't want her to stop talking. Her voice had enveloped me with a warm blanket of comfort and I was in Heaven.

"One day, Pete the orderly was on his way in when something fell out of the sky and landed with a thump on the paving almost beside him. It was a dead and smashed up Dr Waring. It was ruled as an accidental death - or was it suicide? I forget after thirty years, but some of those who knew him well say he was murdered and pushed out the window." Ruthie nodded at me with huge, haunted eyes. She rocked a little as she rubbed her hands together for comfort.

"What did he look like, Ruthie?"

"Young, glasses and he always had Brylcreemed hair. I used to joke with him and tell him he could fry an egg on that head of his."

My heart leapt and I could feel my breathing become rapid. I'd been subconsciously hoping that the concussion had caused a hallucination but Ruthie had quashed those hopes with her accurate description of Dr Waring. She didn't notice my cold sweat or bloodless face as she took my empty bowl and straightened everything around me. She squeezed my hand and breezed out, leaving a faint whiff of Johnson's Baby Lotion behind her.

Joe popped his head around the door not long after Ruthie left. I felt relieved to see him, albeit a little light-headed and aware that my breathing was shallow. I took a few deep breaths and smiled at Joe. He looked dishevelled and flushed. There was a small but noticeable tear in his jumper near the shoulder and his hair was ruffled. Normally, Joe hated to look unkempt.

"What happened, Joe?"

"Oh, nothing. Got into a fight. It was nothing, honestly." He nervously repositioned himself and shifted his gaze to and fro to everything but me. He was keeping something from me. When he finally did make eye contact, the happiness was evident and I forgot to ask him what he was hiding. We chatted and ate the pasta bake his mum had sent, while Joe helped me catch up on what I'd missed at school, including the gossip. I didn't mention Dr Waring. Joe's appearance suggested that he had enough to deal with without a dead medic adding to his concerns.

Christmas was the worst time of year in terms of stress, being on one's best behaviour and having to deal with family members you had managed to avoid all year. It was the time of year we made our annual trip to France to visit our French grandparents. Mum would only allow one suitcase per person, which the owner took full responsibility for. That way she could concentrate on not losing us instead of not losing the luggage.

"Can't wait 'til the tunnel opens. We can take a train then and get there quicker. Don't you think, Tiger?" asked Dad, as he stretched his arms far above his head, a gesture that made him look at least seven foot tall. He always did what he called 'stretch-ing exercises' before embarking upon long drives, looking like a startled pigeon the way he flapped his arms, rotated his wrists and nodded his head simultaneously. He used to do squats too, or 'the constipation move' as Marcus liked to call it, until Mum stopped him, worried that the neighbours would think we were mad.

"Won't it be easier to lose one of us if we took trains, Dad?" I replied, remembering the time I had taken the lift to the roof of the Heathrow airport car park without anyone's knowledge. I'd wanted to be able to touch an aeroplane, thinking that the roof ended in the clouds somewhere. Unfortunately, I had instead sparked a manhunt involving Heathrow security, the police and my frantic parents.

"Alright, smarty-pants. What do we have here?"

I turned my head in the direction of Dad's proud gaze. Vanessa was slowly descending the stairs in true movie star fashion. She had a large woollen shawl draped around her shoul-ders and oversized sunglasses balanced on her perfect nose. I looked down at her feet and knew what was going to happen. She began to totter and, instead of grabbing the banister to steady herself, leaned forward to make sure the pashmina was secure. Luckily, Dad caught her before she hit the floor.

"Can't have our future movie star breaking her lovely nose," Dad said as he propped her up.

Vanessa tucked her fringe behind her ears, trying to appear as nonchalant as possible but already starting to sulk. Mum appeared with a box of food and herded us into the car. I held my breath as Dad reversed straight through a magnificent, ochre shire horse and then we were off. For a fleeting moment I saw Matthew and one of his estate employees waving goodbye as we drove by. My head began to throb gently so I closed my eyes and fell asleep.

My French grandparents were an odd couple in every sense of the word. Grand-Pierre, as our grandfather was called, looked like the farmer that he was, strongly built with tanned, leathery skin and more laughter lines than Dad. He always wore the same coat and cap regardless of the weather. Rather than form coherent words, Grand-Pierre would mumble and end each sentence with a little chuckle. I enjoyed being in his company and getting up early to help him feed the chickens and collect eggs. Over the years he taught me some valuable skills like making butter, preparing a bonfire and understanding animal noises. The moment we arrived I ran straight into his big, safe, welcoming embrace.

On the other hand, Grande-Marie was a completely different kettle of fish. She appeared as if she had just walked off the set of Dynasty with her Hollywood-style manicure, perm and ostentatious jewellery. For some reason she had never called me Genevieve, preferring to refer to me as *le passereau* (the sparrow) instead. It didn't bother me as I hardly listened to her anyway. I would avoid hugging her as she had a bad habit of licking her lips before kissing anyone. Grande-Marie had been very wary of me for the past couple of years. I had once shocked her to her Catholic core by asking what a penis was over Christmas dinner, just as Marcus had recommended I should do. To this day I don't understand why she clucked and flapped the way she did, and for so long too. I mean, it was a perfectly valid question and I was only seven at the time.

I sat at the kitchen table eating cinnamon pancakes and watching Grande-Marie. She was listening intently to Mum as she narrated the story of my head injury, at least her version. Grande-Marie offered no words of advice, sympathy or criticism, preferring to make exaggerated facial expressions and sucking noises every now and again. I noticed how thin her skin was and how the little blood vessels under it made lovely patterns of blue, delicately intertwined like lace. I looked at my hands and wrists and noticed I had the same visible blue network keeping my body alive.

That night I lay awake, too frightened to allow myself the luxury of sleep. Every time I closed my eyes that strange feeling of rushing and distance would compel me to open them again to check that I was still on Earth. I had always been too proud to let myself cry, even when I received the occasional smack, but as I lay in the dark I became overwhelmed by the fear that I would always be like this and the tears flowed anyway.

My mother's sister, Severine, and her brood joined us the next day. By her brood I mean the various dogs and cats that she had adopted to substitute for the children she didn't have and didn't want. Apparently, I had hated her on sight. Dad used to amuse me with stories of my babyhood and how I would wail whenever she was within a twenty-metre radius. He thought I was better than radar and carried me with him so that he knew exactly when to escape.

There was something strange, almost sinister, about Aunt Severine. Whenever Marcus ambled past she would suddenly send out huge tendrils with hooks on the ends that would claw at his stomach and crotch. In fact she did that with most young men. Nearly all of her energy was concentrated around her trunk and belly and was of a sickly green colour that darkened whenever Mum and Vanessa were around. I thought she was the green-eyed monster of jealousy. Aunt Severine's pets resembled a carnival show, dressed in denim, faux suede and diamante, all small, fluffy and vicious. Every year she would set out miniature plates for them full of Christmas dinner, pudding and eggnog, and this year was no exception. When a person wanted to pet them they would be accused of bringing them harm - and then accused of ignoring them after complying with Aunt Severine's wishes. There was simply no winning with her so it was best to avoid her altogether.

Christmas dinner was a very sumptuous and eventful affair, this year topping them all. Mum's brothers, Uncles Philippe and Etien, arrived in the morning with their respective tribes. They were identical twins, married within a month of one another and all their teenage children looked very alike. Marcus fitted in well with our cousins genetically, chronologically and in terms of fashion sense and they were all genuinely happy in each other's company. Aunt Severine's eyes bulged out of their sockets as they feasted on the testosterone-filled scene of youth, which made me feel really uneasy and slightly worried for my brother. Unfortunately for Aunt Severine, Philippe's wife Justine was a bland and nervous woman who was also an excellent judge of character and did not miss a thing. She ensured that Aunt Severine was seated between myself and Grand-Pierre and that her plunging neckline was as far away from the boys as possible. I noted the energies around both of them swelling and dying down accordingly whenever the other moved closer or further away. It was like an invisible stand-off and I prayed that the food would hurry to my end of the table, giving me something to do so I could ignore them.

I busied myself with rearranging my plate of food, trying to make my eating experience as pleasurable as possible. Grande-Marie's gravy was sublime and very alcoholic. It made me feel like I was floating and that everything was worth smiling about, from the kitchen tiles to the cobwebs dangling daintily in the far corner of the room. I must have been very relaxed because I only noticed the signs of obvious anger after Grand-Pierre had served seconds.

There was complete silence at the table barring the occasional murmur from the boys. I looked across the table. Aunt Justine was staring sternly at Aunt Severine, rooted to the spot and full of tension. She was encased in a huge crimson red bubble and a big black spot was swirling around her heart and slowly rising. Aunt Severine's eyes were fixed on Aunt Justine as she sensually peeled away layers of a roast onion and licked her lips mockingly. She looked calm enough but there were large daggers of dark red forming around her, pointing directly at Aunt Justine. Not needing any further indication of what was to happen, I fled to the bathroom. As I shut the door behind me I caught the first filthy lines of a two and a half hour slagging match. Finally, I heard a timid knock on the door. It was Dad.

"You get frightened, Tiger?" he asked, grimacing as he heard yet another swear word being hurled in the background.

"Can we go home, Dad? I want to see if Joe got football boots for Christmas."

This was a blatant lie and I was thankful that Dad had a memory like a sieve when it came to other people's lives. Joe's family did not celebrate Christmas or any other religious festivals. His parents made a huge fuss of birthdays but did not allow religion to be brought into the house in any form. Maybe it was because of the cultural difference that had brought them so much grief and rejection. It didn't matter to me because at that moment I just needed an excuse to go home.

"I'll see what Mum says. She doesn't get to see her parents that often," said Dad gently.

There was another knock on the door as Grand-Pierre poked his head around it, holding out several bottles of beer between his fingers. Dad chuckled as he took one and leaned back against the toilet cistern. Next to enter the bathroom was Marcus and then our cousin Thierry. I watched as they all quickly relaxed and began to enjoy each other's company. Thin, threadlike links formed between them like a giant cobweb that didn't break even as I walked straight through it and out of the door.

The air in the kitchen was thick with resentment and spent anger and I could feel it seeping through my clothes like water. Almost instinctively Mum put her arm around me and marched me outside into the crisp, fresh air.

"Genevieve," she said firmly, "you ran away from the dinner table because you were frightened, it's true?"

I nodded in silent agreement. I was frightened, not of the actual arguing but of the discomfort in the atmosphere. Mum wrapped her cardigan around herself more snugly and folded her arms to keep it in place. She seemed agitated, as though she were struggling to comprehend something much greater than her.

"Genevieve," she began again, "at school, did you run into that wall because someone frightened you, like Severine just did? Are you being bullied?"

"What makes you think that?" I replied, mystified. I couldn't understand how Mum had come to the conclusion that the incident at school was related to the fight between my aunts.

"We asked Joe and he told us about those Blue children and what they've been doing to you and some of the other kids at school. Us parents would like to sort it out before I have to identify you in the morgue." I didn't know what a morgue was and I could not believe Joe had humiliated me by telling my parents about the Blues. My nose began to bleed and Mum let me go back indoors.

During the journey home I began to have an odd sensation in my head that resembled short static explosions interspersed with moments of clarity. My head had felt fine throughout the Christmas break; I had only been a little troubled by the lack of sleep and the occasional headache. But now I was suddenly feeling strange and didn't know why. *Could my ears be damaged as I'd suspected at the hospital?*

As the motorway traffic began to slow down, we eased up next to a long vehicle transporting animals. I could hear them.

Don't be afraid, I've heard it doesn't hurt...

I'll never see my babies again...

I'm so scared...

We'll all be together, don't be afraid.

Why? Why? Why?

They were comforting one another on their way to slaughter. I looked out of the window and caught the soft muzzle of a sheep poking out of the thin air space between slats. Several pairs of forlorn and accepting eyes gazed out at the rolling English countryside.

One last look, one last look, one last look.

As we picked up speed and pulled away, I said a silent prayer for that poor flock of sheep, destined to die at the end of a long, miserable journey. I never ate meat again.

We arrived home just before New Year's Eve and immediately my mind turned to homework and worrying about going back to school. Until then, I had not given a thought to what the other children would think about my 'accident'. Joe came to see me on New Year's Day and Dad took us to feed the ducks at The Basin, the small pond just off Canons Drive.

"Do you think everyone will tease me, Joe?" I was beginning to get anxious.

"Nah. They'd have forgotten by now. Seriously, they won't remember. Pigface and dogface Blue are too thick to remember past yesterday anyway," Joe said, throwing pebbles and bark across the water.

"Why did you tell Mum and Dad about Philip's slap? Were you threatened with detention?"

"Yeah, but it wasn't that." Joe shifted uncomfortably and let his gaze drop to the ground. "Your mum was crying."

It hit me then how worried Mum must have been when she got the telephone call informing her that I'd been taken to hospital. Joe recognised the guilt on my face and reflected the same on his own. I knew how hard it had been for him to tell me, wanting to protect me from the upset that the knowledge would cause me. A part of me wanted to give my mother a big hug and promise never to worry her again; but I knew it was too late for that and a part of her would worry about me incessantly.

"Let's see if you can hit that," Joe said, handing me a pebble and pointing to the island with a weeping willow tree in the middle of The Basin. We sat in silence for a while. Joe stood on the bank throwing pebbles and I propped myself up against one of the trees that had fallen during the 1987 hurricane. I had a good

vantage point to watch what was going on around me. There were several ducks clustered around Dad as he attempted to repair a remote control boat that he'd been given two birthdays ago. He often brought gadgets with him to picnics and trips so that he had something to do. The ducks watched him with curiosity as they quacked amongst themselves, discussing the strange sight before them, trying to guess what the human was doing.

As I shifted my gaze to the trees surrounding the pond, everything seemed to disappear. The houses, cars, pavement... everything melted away and I was left alone by a dimly lit pathway leading to an enormous property in the distance. Gas lamps lighted the pathway and towards the entrance of Canons Drive I could see an imposing gate. Further towards the crossroads was a man herding pigs with a stick. I could make out from his silhouette that it was the same man who had accompanied Matthew when he waved goodbye to me two weeks ago. Behind him loomed The Railway Inn. There were horses tethered outside and lanterns hanging beside the door and by the entrance to the courtyard and beyond. In front of me a carriage stopped briefly by the turnpike and then clattered on, eventually disappearing into the mist. I watched the man inside the turnpike warming his hands by the meagre flame of a solitary candle. He leaned out and caught the bottom of the window frame, slamming it shut and returning his fingers to the warmth and comfort of the tiny flame inside. Something next to the turnpike caught my eye. There was a small gallows next to it. From it dangled what resembled a lumpy, lifeless sack...

"You alright, Tiger?" asked Dad, shattering my concentration and sucking me back to reality. He followed my gaze with his eyes.

"What's in the tree that's bothering you so much?"

"I wanted to see a robin. I've never seen a real, live one before," I lied.

Dad offered me his hand and we started towards home.

"Why did you lie?" whispered Joe in my ear.

"How did you know I was lying?" I whispered back incredulously.

"Because you'd never just stare at a tree waiting for a robin. You'd nick someone's binoculars and go looking, even if you had to plan it for next year. Sometimes I wonder if you see things that I don't."

Ah, but I do, Joe. I wish I could tell you. But if you told me I'm mad and stopped believing in me, I'd be left all alone in my world. Nothing but a human island.

THREE

Outlaws

Policemen don't wear trainers, and those look quite familiar.

The first day of the spring term was as horrendous a day in the life of any bullying victim as could be. I was teased mercilessly and accused of being brain damaged, mad or cursed. To make matters worse, I had won two national story-writing competitions and my artwork had been chosen for next year's Christmas card by a large charity. The jealousy I encountered from everybody shoved me from every direction and made my energy contract to the point where I felt I had no buffer. Most of the class agreed that I must be a witch and made crossed finger signs every time I looked over at any of them.

"You and your mum did voodoo on the story judges, didn't you, freak?" hissed Daniella from the adjacent table.

"My mum said she ran into the wall because one of her spells went wrong," offered the greasy child who sat next to her. She was abnormally spotty for a ten year old and I later found out that she was actually eleven but was forced to repeat the year because she was 'educationally challenged'. The whole table began to giggle and flick rubbers at me. Some of them hit my face and really hurt. I spent the rest of the day fighting back tears and wishing that I were anywhere else in the world but school.

By some miracle, I was left alone the next day. There was no name-calling, rubber-throwing, shoving or any other form of bullying directed at me. I became increasingly aware that my fellow pupils were actually trying to avoid me, making me inwardly relieved and more relaxed by the time the register was called out. Joe was absent that morning and many of my classmates looked bruised and battered. I was a little confused at first, wanting to know what I'd missed, but then realised that, as long as I were left alone, ignorance really was bliss. During Assembly I began to feel funny. It started off as a faint, high-pitched sound in my ears, followed by light-headedness. On the wall I could see a scene being played out, almost like watching a silent movie. In it Philip Blue and other members of the class were lying in wait for someone in the bushes in Camrose Park. They had a pair of garden shears with them. Joe and two members of the school football team crept up behind them and caught them off-guard. A huge fight ensued and…

"Genevieve, it's time to stand up to go!" whispered Mrs Harmon desperately. I looked up to find everybody looking down at me. I jumped up and whispered back, "Mrs Harmon, Joe didn't tell me he'd be away today. I'm a bit worried. Do you know anything?"

"See me after Assembly," she replied, patting my shoulder gently.

Mrs Harmon stood before me, grey from head to foot, clasping her hands as though her fingers were in danger of falling off. She looked like a cross between a librarian and a dancer and I wanted to ask her if she used to practise walking with a book on her head. She explained that Joe and Philip were with the head teacher because they'd been involved in a fight the day before. Sullen and heavy, I meandered through the cluster of children and desks and plonked myself down on my chair. Joe was fighting because of me, I realised sadly.

Later that morning I was called in to see the head teacher. I was a regular visitor to the Head's office for both academic achievement and discipline. Generally, I knew beforehand what the reason was and what to expect. Not this time, however. As my footsteps echoed and bounced off the surfaces of the corridor I tried to make sense of the confusion I was feeling. It was a wasted effort, with every attempt to find a reason I ended up confusing myself more. Just as I approached the door I froze in horror. I could hear voices within and one of them belonged to Mum.

What the hell have I done now? Why is she here? I'll be grounded for the next thirty years, I just know it.

I knocked on the door with great trepidation, my heart threatening to burst through my ribcage and land with a wet splat on the drab, concrete floor. The door creaked open to reveal a row of faces, all staring at me. I could sense that a battle of wills was taking place; I was not directly to blame but involved never-theless. I scanned the faces in front of me: Philip Blue and his equally pug-faced parents, Joe and his parents, another two couples and a lone woman I didn't recognise, and Mum and Dad. Both Joe and Philip were injured – Joe had a fat lip and a black eye and Philip's nose was broken. I took a seat next to Dad who held my hand the moment I sat down. Although I knew that I wasn't in trouble, I could not relax knowing that the fight I had somehow seen had been real. There was a long pause before the head teacher spoke.

"Genevieve, it turns out that these two young men were fighting because of you. Ordinarily, that would be a very flattering gesture. However, on this occasion it seems that Philip here was lying in wait with some garden shears in order to cut your hair."

"It wasn't just me!" Philip called out, jumping up indignantly and waving a chubby fist in the air.

"Sit down!" his father bellowed, deflating Philip's bravado instantly. I concentrated on his wobbling double chin and he began to scratch it with dirty, flattened fingernails.

"I have also been led to believe that Philip has been making life difficult for you for some time now. And this led to the bump on your head before Christmas."

"Bump on the head? She was in hospital, concussed!" cried Mum.

"Quiet, Eloise, there are children in the room too," said Dad in a low voice.

"I can assure you, Mrs Kelly, that I take bullying very seriously and I intend to stamp it out…"

I was finding it increasingly difficult to remain focussed on the conversation and my mind wandered off to the cream cheese and apple sandwiches in my lunchbox. Joe was willing me to turn round, I could sense it, but I didn't dare to at that moment for fear that I would react in some way.

Joe and I sat opposite one another in the dining room, unpacking our lunches in silence. I laid out my array of goodies in the order in which I intended to eat them. My eyes were still bleary and red from crying. Saying goodbye to Mum and Dad had been very difficult for reasons that I couldn't fathom. The very thought of being unprotected for a few hours was too much to bear and I had burst into tears. They'd had to leave me howling by the front entrance until one of the welfare ladies shoved a tissue in my hand and guided me back inside. But I was not entirely unprotected. I had Joe. I watched him now, sucking juice through a straw that disappeared into his fat lip. Gazing lovingly at Joe over a meal would be one of the simple pleasures of my young life that I would take for granted for many years to come, although I could never have guessed that at the time.

"Joe," I said. My voice sounded small and feeble. "Thank you."

Joe rolled his eyes and attacked his sandwich with gusto. He did not look up from his plate again, neither did he pause between mouthfuls to breathe or digest. A minute later three of his football buddies seated themselves around us. They struck up a conversation centred on the beautiful game and I switched off, preferring to watch Joe as the nucleus of it, truly in his element. I stared at him for a long time as I retreated into a bubble of pale green and yellow, cocooning myself from the world around me. The blackness around Joe's stomach began to dissipate as his friends made him laugh out loud. As I watched the dark wisps float by, I could see fleeting scenes of violence as Joe threw punches, blinded by an uncontrollable rage.

At home time I was made to wait with a member of staff for Vanessa to come and escort me home. I watched as children and parents milled around, sometimes bouncing off one another like energised particles in a physics experiment. That day there was football practice in the afternoon but Joe had been temporarily relegated to the substitutes' bench as punishment. I felt a pang of guilt as I watched him slumped on the side lines in his tracksuit and gloves.

"Is that your sister? Gosh, isn't she tall and lovely!" exclaimed the teacher beside me. Vanessa was striding towards me waving a gloved hand. She was taller than some of the parents and appeared much healthier than everyone else due to her perennial tan. Her height made her appear older than she was and she displayed none of the awkwardness of other adolescents her age. There was not a shred of similarity between us other than our voices. Some of the boys in the football team stopped playing to gawp at her and the rest collided with them.

"Shall we get going?" she said, swinging her head from side to side to get the hair away from her face. Vanessa was lucky, she had straight and silky curtains that didn't break comb teeth or get caught on foliage like mine did. I had spent most of my young life trying to tame my wild barnet. I realised I was staring into space and blinked as Vanessa noticed and shouted at me.

"No offence, Genevieve, but can you walk a bit behind me? It's really sad to walk with a junior, even if we are related." Saying nothing, I fell into step keeping my eyes fixed on Vanessa's coltish legs and wishing that either Joe or Dad were there to entertain me.

The rest of the winter was uneventful with undertones of resentment and unpleasantness at school which played havoc with my digestion. Philip was suspended and then moved to another class while Daniella and company were placed under surveillance. I was assigned a pastoral care tutor to whom I had to report every Friday morning for ten minutes. It was an easy way to waste ten minutes as I had very little to say.

As the New Year continued, I spent increasing amounts of time outdoors, watching the bands of movement around the trees and feeling the heartbeat of the ground beneath my feet. *So this is how you all communicate.*

It was during these intervals of blissful solitude that I would allow the torrents of tears to gush down my face and cleanse my being both inside and out. I was also able to reflect sadly on how I still struggled to find any sort of niche. My personal relationships had deteriorated as my family and peers stopped trying to understand me and started to judge me instead, the latter choice requiring less effort. I was as alien to them as they were to me and, try as I might, I could find no middle ground. The only constants in my life were Joe and Dad, although even he was obviously frustrated at the fact that he couldn't communicate with or recognise his own daughter anymore. It seemed to hurt him more that he never witnessed me crying or showing any signs of distress or emotion.

The truth was that I was completely empty by the time I came home and had constructed an invisible barrier that I would reinforce with each small breakdown of strength. Inevitably, I became a loner with no tangible human friends of my own age other than Joe. The reality was that I had John Graham, Matthew and all the abundant flora and fauna outside.

Far from being a safe haven, my bedroom became the place where I had to be most vigilant. I was painfully aware of my mother's presence outside once I had closed the door, waiting to eavesdrop on any conversations I may have with 'myself'. The garden was often the place where John Graham and I could play in peace, as it was impossible to spy on us from the house without leaving the back door or an upstairs window obviously open for the purpose.

When it was dry I ventured into Canons Park and would often bump into Matthew there. I sometimes begged John Graham to come with me but he would refuse, without explanation and with a knowing look in his eyes. Had I been old enough to comprehend the concept of fate, I would have known that the two were destined never to meet or to have any link between them other than me and the land they both held dear.

As the months flew by, I came to think of myself as Matthew's apprentice. He taught me about horses, how to groom them a certain way to provide massage to their muscles, how to decipher their different neighs and snorts, how to appreciate their magnificence by ensuring they got what they needed. He refused to teach me how to ride, though, explaining that I was far too small and shire horses respected a weightier load. He described the various injuries men had sustained falling from their great heights and so I was happy to wait, trusting his judgement completely. To be honest, cleaning poo from the stable floor was preferable to going home and the monotonous action of constant shovelling was a form of meditation in itself. Matthew even built me a small stepladder out of the wood of fallen branches that had been scattered around the estate after a terrible storm the previous winter. He let me help him smooth the wood with a huge file and sit on the planks to weigh them down as he sawed them. I used the stepladder for many years to groom velvety flanks and to pick apples, until it became lost in time like millions of objects before and after it.

Dad and I walked up the steep incline towards Harrow School. I was not a fan of Harrow viewpoint, thinking it to be haunted, but we had often had family picnics there and Dad thought walking there would help reduce his middle age spread.

"Dad, what's Morg?"

"Eh?"

"What's Morg?"

"What do you mean? A morgue, m-o-r-g-u-e?"

"Not sure, but Mum says she might see me there one day. What is it?"

"Ah! I'll have to speak to Mum about this…"

"Daaaad, what is it?"

"Well, it's where dead people are kept."

"Why?"

"So that they can be examined to make sure their families know exactly how they died and then they can be prepared for cremation or burial. Sometimes, if there's some uncertainty about who the dead person is, family members have to go there to identify them."

"Like in Quincy?"

"Exactly."

"Cool. I can't wait to end up in a morgue."

"Oi, oi, oi. That's a long way away. You're probably going to be here until you're ninety or something. Remember that."

"Thirty-one. That's the number I keep coming up with."

"Thirty-one what?"

"I'll be here until I'm thirty-one."

"How can you be so sure?"

"I just know. Like I know my hair is dark."

"And what will happen to you at thirty-one that's so bad that you'll end up in the morgue?"

"Um… cancer."

"Oh."

"Dad, what's cancer?"

"Never mind. I'll tell you when you're older. Let's not have this conversation again, okay?" Neither one of us mentioned it again.

One Sunday in late spring I woke up feeling very disorientated. The sun was brighter than usual and I wondered how Mum could have used the bathroom without waking me up with the noise. The hallway and staircase looked different and I blinked several times to make sure I was truly awake. *The walls were apricot white yesterday…* Panic gripped me as I realised I was in somebody else's house and had no idea how I'd got there.

There was a gruff cough in the living room and the sound of something hard being placed gently on a shiny surface. I peered around the door and met the gaze of a man I'd never seen before. He beckoned for me to sit down on a chaise longue by the door and I complied, completely at ease now. He had a tender gaze and fatherly mannerisms and I couldn't help wondering why he appeared to be so familiar to me when I was sure I'd never seen him before. I observed him and his fascinating familiarity. He got up and went to the fireplace, leaning against it as he took something from a tiny, ornate soapstone box and putting it up his nostrils, inhaling roughly. He was a good-looking man, with bearing rather than being conventionally handsome, somewhere on the flattering side of forty. The light streaming in through the bay window caught his fading ginger hair and transformed it into a neat copper halo. He sat down in an armchair and began filling a large pipe. As he smiled at me, the corners of his orange moustache lifted and his crystal blue eyes shone. This was Michael Davis, John Graham's father.

The silence between the two of us was full of invisible, hovering communications. Michael Davis looked kind and brimming with proper old-fashioned gentility. He was comfortable in his starched collar and his own skin and seemed the type of person children and animals would be drawn to. Sitting with him now I felt my initial panic subside and we spent a pleasant few minutes looking at each other across the room. He did not look like his son but there was an unmistakable resemblance and the smile was uncanny. He lit a match and put it to the fat end of his pipe, sucking and pupping as he did so. I watched with amusement as his moustache and eyebrows jumped up and down with the action.

The living room was a cavern of exotic treasures and rich materials, the centrepiece a deep pile ornamental rug of rich greens and browns, twisting and turning to create a magnificent tropical design. A Chinese paper screen stood in the corner by the bay window, throwing splashes of multi-coloured light up the wall. Numerous Indian paintings adorned the walls making it difficult to catch any regular pattern of the wallpaper underneath. Apart from the various curios on display, everything else was definitely occidental and of the finest quality and taste. It was a cosy room rather than a cluttered one and the miscellany around me somehow all lent itself to producing a delightful haven for a well-travelled philanthropist or a curious young mind. I smiled to myself as I pictured John Graham playing out imaginary games and scenarios with his father's nick-knacks.

I faced Michael Davis once more and found him watching me with a half-smile on his face. He nodded and I nodded back.

Then a huge uncontrollable yawn escaped my mouth and in the split second that I closed my eyes Michael Davis was gone. All that remained of him was the smell of his tobacco lingering in my nostrils and the multi-coloured imprint of his orange halo in my field of vision.

I had decided time and again to tell Joe about John Graham but sure enough I failed to do so. This was partly due to the stress at school and home, and partly to my own hesitation. My friendship with Joe was the only source of security that I felt I had, now that my family had passed judgement, and I could not afford to lose it. Joe himself was struggling to maintain a certain, basic level of self-esteem in the formidable shadow of his good-looking, charming and academically gifted older brother and I could not add to his burden. In the summer, Ravi had gained twelve A-grades in his O Levels and the pressure was on for Joe to equal or surpass his record. It was unfortunate that Joe's real talents were overlooked in favour of an unattainable, conventionally successful version of him. Nobody said anything when Joe was made captain of the school football team or when he represented the county in three different track and field events. Nobody, that is, except me. As the years went by, Joe become more and more angry; unless his achievements reminded his parents of Ravi, they simply didn't notice.

The bullying became progressively worse until Daniella was also suspended for trying to break my fingers by shutting them in a desk drawer. Unfortunately for her, Joe did not believe that girls should be exempt from playground punishment and Daniella soon found she was missing a couple of teeth. Being female, and an egotistical one at that, Daniella sought revenge. One lunch break I found myself knocked to the floor and pinned down while Daniella succeeded in completing the job that Philip was unable to finish. I spent the rest of the summer covering my shapeless frizzy hair with caps, bandanas and large headbands, wondering when it was going to end and I would be left alone.

To my dismay, Mum joined in the fight and lodged a formal complaint with the school governors, my endless pleading about fighting my own battles falling on deaf ears. I may as well have had leprosy, as nobody wanted to associate with me after hearing that my mother had come in to stand up for my rights and almost shouted the place down.

Mrs Harmon sprang a series of surprise tests on us in June. She claimed that they were nothing to be afraid of, occurred annually and would assist her in deciding which groups we would be in for Maths and English next year. I noticed that the energy around her changed the moment she said they were nothing to worry about, obscuring her from view. This worried me. She was lying.

A few days later I was summoned to the head teacher's office for no apparent reason whatsoever. I was sure it had something to do with those tests and convinced myself that I was going to be accused of cheating, so I had to come up with a good defence before I reached the office of doom. I gulped my heart back down as I approached. Then my mother's voice permeated through the cracks in the door frame before I had reached out to grab the handle. *Not again.* I sighed and let my shoulders drop a few inches before I walked through the door.

Apparently, I was not in trouble at all but quite the opposite. The head teacher was gesticulating wildly and raving about how well I was doing and how the school could have its first Mensa child and how it had been years since a former pupil of the school attended Oxbridge. I knew what Oxbridge was because of Marcus.

"Mum, who's Mensa?"

"Well Genevieve, it's like a special club for clever children like you. It seems that you did very well in your tests." She beamed at me, which was disconcerting because my mother never beamed; normally she scowled or frowned. I watched her closely. Her energy bubble was a pale green today and kept flickering like a light bulb on its last legs. She was relieved and nervous.

"Oh," I said, unimpressed by all the fuss. "What kind of club is it? Can I read there?"

"Genevieve," said the head teacher with the enthusiasm of a children's television presenter. "Well done! You've scored a reading and writing age of sixteen and three-quarters. That's marvellous for a ten year old, don't you think?"

"But what kind of club is it?" I was beginning to lose interest, my mind wandering to the contents of my lunchbox. *I wonder what drink Dad has given me today. It had better not be orange juice, or OJ as Marcus calls it. I don't care what vitamin C is, it's got no right to force its way into my meals the way it does.*

"Genevieve, answer the question!" hissed Mum between clenched teeth.

"Huh? I don't want to commit myself either way at this stage." *There! That's diplomatic enough to cover most questions.*

The bell rang for break and I was dismissed. As I left I had the feeling that the adults were plotting something without my knowledge. I was not wrong. Over the summer my parents had a few clandestine meetings with the relevant parties at school and in September I found myself being forced to join the year above.

It was obvious that I was considered a social outcast from the moment I entered the classroom and sat down at the only empty desk. Although nobody was staring at me directly, I could sense them poking and prodding me in a subtle, invisible way. They were curious and offended by my presence at the same time. There was a big-boned girl with very long hair like Vanessa's sitting next to me. She looked older than everybody else and I noticed that she had very sad and lonely eyes. There was a small kidney bean bobbing around her abdomen, towards the periphery of her bubble, which turned very dark at times. Something about her bothered me but I couldn't put my finger on it so I ignored the feeling and turned to face her.

"You look too small to be here," she stated, as she scrutinised my appearance unashamedly. I felt vulnerable and wriggled a little.

"I got moved here. Thing is, I'd rather be back where I was. I don't care about the bullying, I don't feel very comfortable…" I stopped to gulp, aware that there were tears welling up in my eyes and that my voice had risen an octave.

"At least you're going up. I got moved down," said the girl. She separated a lock from the rest of her hair, twisted it and sucked it. "It's `cos I'm thick. I don't get anything." *Why would anyone say that about themselves?*

"I can help you with your homework if you like," I offered, partly out of pity and partly out of the need to do something before I cracked up in her face. Although there was something uncomfortable sitting in the pit of my stomach, I had a feeling that we were going to be friends. I looked at her, marvelling at how anybody could be so naturally uncouth.

"I'm Mongo, by the way. After that big thick one in the Heathcliff cartoons."

"I'm Genevieve. Please don't call me Gene."

We shook hands and turned around as our new class teacher walked in and rapped a ruler on his desk.

I hated every minute of being in the year above. The children were hateful and they made it clear that none of them would associate with me for fear of being branded as the babysitter. The only exception was Mongo, who warded off teasing and ridicule by virtue of her superior stature and a penchant for punching her left hand with her right fist as she looked at someone. It amused me how she mispronounced my name, settling for Jenny-Veeve, and offered to carry my books to the school exit at home time. I told Joe and his friends that we had become a regular George and Lenny, although most of them didn't understand the reference at the time.

I missed Joe and we would still eat lunch together, but for the rest of the day I felt like a misfit. He also walked me home almost every day and would wait for me without fail. I noticed how his face would darken when he saw Mongo and how he rarely acknowledged her verbally when she was present. The strange thing was that the moment his energy started to grow denser, it would also grow huge, enveloping me within it and creating a barrier between me and Mongo. He would whisk me away from her as quickly as he could and only allow his shoulders to relax when we were at a safe distance.

"Joe, why don't you like Mongo?" I ventured to ask one afternoon as we competed to kick the same pebble home.

"She's dodgy. I don't trust her," he said, scowling at nothing in particular.

"Why?"

"Just… dunno… I feel it here," he patted his abdomen a few times. "I wish you were back in class, you know. I can't muck around with anyone else. It's just not the same."

His head hung low and the air around him went grey and musty; he was utterly dejected. Joe and I never had to use superfluous explanations, we just understood one another. I knew exactly how he felt.

We spent most of the winter together either plotting ways to get me demoted or finding new activities through which to channel his anger and alleviate my frustration. My sense of being different had made me feel increasingly isolated until I was unable to speak to anyone about anything, apart from Joe. I had become a human archipelago, very nearly an island but with a fragile lifeline to the mainland. From the isolation stemmed an irrational fear of losing Joe and a sense of ennui that seeped into the core of me and became entrenched there. I lost all interest in fitting in and accepted the role of the outsider. There were times when I wished that somebody, anybody, would notice me and tell me that it was alright to be the way I was and that I was safe being different. But nobody did. That's why, during those cold winter days, Joe and I thought long and hard about things we could do to express ourselves. Eventually we took up vandalism and burglary.

Most Friday nights, Mum and Dad entertained their friends at home and Mum made sure we were fed and sent to bed early. Marcus was dispatched to the cinema with some money. It was the perfect opportunity to escape via my bedroom window, roof and drainpipe for a few hours. As long as I was back by half past eleven, clean and injury free, I knew I was safe. It was never our intention to harm anyone, so Joe and I would very carefully consider what we were going to do and plan each 'sting' in advance. Sometimes we had to 'borrow' equipment and the challenge of returning it undamaged and on time only added to the excitement. We had some really good times executing ingenious plots, and it was during this period that our maturing energy patterns started to become entwined, creating a dependence relationship that would last until I died.

My favourite spree was the one where I had to squeeze through a ventilation shaft in order to steal a can of paint before painting an 'I' in the middle of as many To Let signs as I could within an hour. It was the perfect masterpiece blitz and timed to military precision. I even managed to preserve the empty can and put it back before returning home. Only its lack of weight would have given it away, but who was going to notice that when it was sitting on a shelf? The next week, everybody at school was talking about it and wondering who the vandal could be. For the first time ever, my heart swelled with pride but I said nothing. It was our secret, Joe's and mine.

It got worse still and I began to use what Joe called my 'sixth sense' to ensure there was nobody around to catch us. It was easy, as all I had to do was look for the energy imprint that everybody leaves behind. To this day I remember the feeling of being alive, challenged and carefree. Maybe it was the lack of sleep that had numbed my conscience, or maybe I had totally lost my place as a member of a society I felt no part of. But I am sure that if I had experienced just an ounce of understanding then, my life would have taken a completely different course.

The only problem with enjoying a challenge was that every successive challenge had to be greater than the one preceding it, for it to have the same effect. It was inevitable, then, that one of our bright ideas would be our undoing. As the days grew longer, Joe and I were forced to execute increasingly daring plans in a more limited time frame. We were caught just before Fathers' Day. Joe thought it would be a great idea to target the Blues as well as having some fun along the way. We decided to steal a 'Humps for $^2/_3$ of a mile' sign and tie it to their front gate. Earlier that evening, I managed to 'borrow' some of Dad's tools and wrapped them individually in cloth so that they wouldn't clink together, before tying them around my lower legs for portability.

I'd had a bad feeling about the expedition since making our plans on the prior Tuesday, but I'd ignored my gut feeling this time, giving in to the overwhelming temptation. Running at our usual pace proved difficult with the weight of the tools so we had to work quickly once we arrived at the chosen sign.

Because I had to stand on Joe's back to remove the bolts, it was impossible not to look suspicious and our problem was exacerbated by my strength being no match for the tightness of the bolts. Joe had the bright idea of standing on the bonnet of an adjacent parked car, which promptly set off the car's alarm and sent us scurrying away like disturbed mice. Making a getaway over brick walls and through back gardens was what got us caught. Normally we had the presence of mind to consider carefully the pitfalls of any escape route. This time we were so panic stricken that common sense deserted us.

Joe had already scaled a wall and was waiting, perched at the top, for me to follow. But the tools were weighing me down so much that I simply could not lift my legs high enough to swing myself up. Sensing somebody approaching, Joe and I became frantic. He grabbed my arms as I grappled with the wall, dislodging my grip and sending us both tumbling onto the cold pavement where I found myself face to face with a pair of worn Adidas trainers. *Policemen don't wear trainers,* I thought without an ounce of relief, *and those look quite familiar.*

It was Dad, looking stony faced and livid. He grabbed me by the scruff of my neck and Joe by the ear and marched us home where we were greeted with a stinging slap each from Mum.

"What is wrong with you?" Mum yelled as soon as Joe had gone. "What is your problem? You're turning into a delinquent for no real reason!" I didn't answer but listened to her voice. It interested me how Mum's French accent would emerge when she was angry and how her Rs became increasingly guttural with rage.

"It's that boy's fault!" she wailed. That annoyed me and I let her know it.

"It's your fault. I'm angry with you. I hate my class, nobody will speak to me because I'm the clever dick and you never listen."

I stopped as soon as I realised that I'd said the word 'dick' in front of my mother. I braced myself for another slap but it didn't come. Instead she waved her hand to dismiss me and I went to bed feeling lonely, wondering how Joe was getting on and whether Mum would put me in foster care.

FOUR

Team Player

*Had I dreamt all of that? Sometimes I wish
Mum would shut up.*

I had started to tutor Mongo in the autumn so that she could catch up and she was making some progress with her reading. At first I wondered if she had some kind of learning impairment, but there was no confusion around her at all when she tried to read - she simply couldn't do it. I would often watch her as she concentrated hard on pronouncing words, her scrunched up forehead barely visible behind the thick mass of cloudiness that was a permanent feature in front of her face. Sometimes it would twist together a bit like a unicorn's horn just before she threw the book on the floor and crossed her arms in anger. Secretly, I thanked my lucky stars that I had not been born stupid – at least I could hide my weirdness and pretend I was normal. Still, Mongo didn't give up and I did admire her determination.

Eventually she was able to read. With her excitement at being able to string a sentence together came a new-found sense of power that she exercised mercilessly. Knowing what it was like to be bullied, I tried to reason with her but to no avail. She seemed really to enjoy breaking Mark's glasses and stealing Ruth's dinner money and finding cruel ways of adding insult to the injuries she inflicted. It bothered me that she seemed to have no conscience and it dawned on me that associating with her so closely meant that my classmates were even less likely to talk to me. By now the reality was that unless Mongo was at school, which she often was not, I didn't have a PE partner or somebody to walk to Assembly with. I was the last person to be picked for any sports team without exception and the classroom would always become quiet when I entered in the morning. I knew that I was different and I didn't mind being considered unacceptable by most, but this kind of sustained treatment made me feel like there was something so wrong with me that I didn't even merit one jot of respect. The only member of that class who held me in any regard was Mongo and by default I grew to trust her as much as I trusted Joe.

One day as we walked towards Burnt Oak Broadway where Mongo lived, I decided that I needed to tell someone and blurted it all out. She listened intently while we waited in the queue at Munchy's; she ate her steaming chips and looked at the window display at Anthony's Drugstore as was her normal home time ritual. She didn't say a word, nor did she ask me any questions.

There! I've told someone! Congratulations, Genevieve, for overcoming your lack of trust!

Later at home I felt lighter and freer than I had for years and it was apparent in my mood. Mum remarked at the wonderful transformation of her normally morose and surly youngest and felt that it was down to either Jesus or the onset of menstruation. I did feel a little guilty about not telling Joe first, but I didn't allow it to affect my mood that weekend. Joe would be told the whole truth when I next saw him alone.

My greatest achievement turned out to be my biggest mistake. At school on Monday, Mongo's bullying had found a new direction and focus: me. What really hurt was that we had been such good friends but that seemed to hold absolutely no weight with her. I spent most days dodging darts of hatred and being probed on an energetic level. It made me tired in more ways than one and I began to make plans to escape as soon as I could.

"You're a real weirdo, Jenny-Veeve!"

"Why? Just because I'm different to you?"

"No, it's 'cos I say so. Lots of people say so. You're a witch what speaks to ghosts."

"Who's going to tutor you now?"

"My new friends. Normal people, innit."

They did not bother tutoring her and by the end of summer term she had reverted to being bottom of the class again.

Over the summer, Mum and Dad had spoken to the head teacher and I was readmitted to my proper year group on the condition that I had private tuition in addition to my normal lessons to keep me challenged and happy. The talk of my so-called madness had now reached the psychologist, and I was to maintain my sessions with the tutor on Fridays to ensure that the bullying was kept in check. But the pastoral care was soon rendered defunct and all the bullying directed at me ceased immediately because of a miracle of nature: Vanessa had grown boobs over the summer. They were not just any boobs but full C cup balloons that augmented her other blooming womanly curves and above average stature. Her popularity soared, as did mine by association. Suddenly all the boys started being polite to me and the girls acknowledged me as human, all because they feared offending Vanessa in some way and thus forfeiting their piece of her status at school. It was intriguing to say the least. Vanessa's bubble suddenly swelled with confidence and every time she walked down the corridor it would merge momentarily with the kids' bubbles as they stopped to look at her or greet her. She would then snap away from them like an elastic band and their bubbles would become momentarily forlorn and droopy as she walked away, almost consciously enjoying what she was doing to them. I had never seen anything quite like it.

Vanessa began to change. Her arguments with Mum and Dad increased with frequency and intensity. She took up smoking as a form of rebellion and weight management and gave up her pursuit of Ravi, branding him 'a boring old swot'. Her colours changed too. She was now mainly a dark red because she was angry so often and there was a similar cloudiness to that of Marcus around her head. It was difficult to remain in the same room as her due to the feeling of being stifled or overpowered by her anger. I would often fight to breathe in her presence. One thing that did not change was her embarrassment of me. She very rarely admitted that we were related and never invited me anywhere, even to her own birthday parties. She complained to Mum about the shame she felt at my straggly appearance and insisted that I ought either to be sent to France to learn how to dress or put in an asylum. But her outbursts could not bother me for long. The moment I began to feel over-whelmed or frustrated I would climb out of the window, across the roof, along the fence and run to Joe's home or to Canons Park.

It was a secondary miracle that Vanessa's beauty did nothing to erode my own self-esteem. In fact, I was oblivious to it which irritated her to the point of attack. The black darts would start flying out of her throat and stomach, as her fists began to curl and a sinister inkiness seeped out of her torso. It would swirl a bit before pooling around her throat and then she would have to get rid of it by swearing at me. The thing she could not understand was that a person's outward appearance was only of interest to me in an academic way. Beauty and ugliness were on par with one another in my eyes – I found them equally fascinating and was just as likely to appreciate a malformed genetic mess as a radiant model of perfect proportion. It was the way people made me feel that made me notice them; it was whether they repelled or attracted me invisibly that counted. I found more pleasure in twiddling my heartstrings around lanky and awkward Joe than trying to make some kind of connection with Vanessa at any level.

What exactly is beautiful anyway? Joe's nose is lovely and Mum says it looks like a beak. And why are my feet so freakish to people? I like having big feet – they anchor me when it's windy. I admired my feet. They had grown before the rest of me and I spent two years dragging them around rather than walking with a normal gait. My sister didn't have a gait but seemed to glide everywhere in the comfort of her inflated bubble. I would often observe Vanessa's movements to try and see the beauty in her, but all I could see were the pursed lips, the hatred of anything she deemed to be beneath her and the permanent scowl etched on her face.

My cast-iron confidence was first brought to my attention by Dr Steward, the Educational Psychologist, who believed none of it and accused me of being secretly jealous of my sister. Our first meeting on a very rainy Thursday in March was a disaster, as were all our subsequent appointments. I'm sure I played an indirect part in the stress-related heart attack that killed him four years later. Mum insisted on accompanying me to each appointment so that she could keep abreast of what was going on. Every time we would leave Dr Steward feeling exasperated and in desperate need of a drink. I knew which visits he had prepared for with a tot or two – it was clear from the haze that surrounded him just how much he had had already although my mother never seemed to notice. He asked some very stupid questions and I found myself giving the most ridiculous answers just for the amusement of watching the haziness become active with his exasperation.

"Genevieve, can you tell me why you're here?"

"I don't know, you're supposed to tell me, aren't you?"

"How do you feel about your sister being so tall and beautiful?"

"Erm, well, I don't feel like getting plastic surgery, if that's what you're asking."

"Does bullying affect you negatively, in your opinion?"

"Well, no, I look forward to it every day."

"Why do you think you see things, Genevieve?"

"Because I'm not blind. Is that a trick question?"

Eventually he had to make a diagnosis, partly to avoid the humiliation of conceding defeat and partly to get me off his patient list before I gave him a nervous breakdown.

"ADHD, Mrs Kelly."

"What's that?" asked Mum, a little louder than she meant to. I could hear her breathing become a touch more rapid.

"It's a type of hyperactivity disorder, an attention deficit that affects children. Concentration spans are short so they cannot pay attention as well as normal children. Emotional stress makes it worse so the school bullying will most likely be making it worse, as does Genevieve's diet."

My diet? He's never even asked me once what I eat.

"What do we do?" Mum's breathing had slowed down again but she was wringing her hands together constantly. Her hands were rough with thick skin under which you couldn't see the veins. They were not smooth and translucent like mine and her fingers were robust-looking with slightly spatulate tips. I used to love watching them knead dough when I was very little.

Practical hands like in Cheiro's book.

"I don't think Genevieve's ADHD is bad enough to warrant the use of drugs but you will have to train her to pay attention for longer and don't give her any stimulants like sweets or coffee. A firm hand might work wonders."

Dr Steward's last comment had visibly irritated Mum and I half expected her to hit him. She didn't but instead shook his hand so tightly that he had to shake some of the pain out of it afterwards. Mum grabbed my arm and marched me down the corridor almost too fast for my shorter legs to cope with.

"But I don't eat sweets or drink coffee, Mum. You won't let me."

"Firm hand, my arse," I heard her mutter. She said 'arse' with an Irish accent, like Dad did. "We'll get a second opinion from elsewhere."

"Can't everyone just leave me alone?" I whined. I had become fed up with the long drives to Dr Steward's London office after school. They meant I had to sit up late doing homework and go to bed later too. I was only ten when the sessions had started and I just wanted to be a normal child for a change. Mum's eyes softened a little and we drove home in silence.

John Graham and I sat in the garden facing a chilly wind that October, discussing siblings and my ADHD.

"They think you're mad, Genevieve?" he asked, wide-eyed and adorably cute. I used to wish sometimes that I'd been born adorably cute, just to see how different people's reactions towards me would be. Then I realised that for me to remain that way would have required too much effort and I simply could not be bothered to maintain such a high level of fallacy. I was not naturally cute and everybody, including myself, just had to deal with it.

"Probably."

"Will they send you away to an asylum?"

"No, they sent me to Mensa, which was strange and a bit boring. I had to sit lots of tests but they were pointless so I ran out of patience and started drawing horses on the sheets when I finished answering the questions. Vanessa thinks I should be sent away because she's ashamed of me."

"What's Mensa?"

"A children's club, I think, but I didn't actually meet any other children there. It looked more like a government facility. Actually, it was more friendly than that. I wonder if they injected a tracking device into my brain while I was there." I scratched my scalp to check. John Graham looked lost when I started talking about tracking devices.

"Why would your parents send you to a children's club? Is it a 'funny' club? We have a relative in an asylum that nobody talks about. I'm not even sure what their name is or what they are exactly. I only know this because my aunt brings it up sometimes to frighten us with." He shuddered as he said the last part.

"I don't see the shame or stigma in being bonkers. Mad people are just people who see and do things differently because that's how they're wired. Sounds interesting to me. Anyway, how do we know it's them that are mad and not us? Because we're in the majority?"

"But they're outcasts - and dangerous too." John Graham was struggling and I remembered that he was much younger than I was and more sheltered.

"Do I look dangerous to you, John Graham?" I asked softly.

"No."

"Well then."

"If you're sent away, then I'm coming too!" he shouted at nobody in particular. "Oh look! There's my mother!"

I looked in the general direction of his pointed finger. A buxom and well-dressed woman in her mid-thirties came out of the back door with a large empty basket. I watched her as she hitched up her skirts a little and knelt on the ground to pick up the apples that had fallen onto the lawn. She was a pretty woman rather than beautiful, with a fresh complexion and the same rosy cheeks as her son. Her dark blonde hair was pinned into a loose knot at the nape of her long neck. Some loose strands fell into her eyes as she plucked an excited and squirming John Graham from the ground and hugged him tightly. She had a wonderfully throaty and feminine laugh that filled the garden and took a decade off her face. Margaret Davis beckoned to me with a long, white finger and a warm, welcoming smile and I complied, falling into step behind her and her beloved son. Just before we reached the back door, Margaret Davis knelt down, stroked my hair away from my face and said:

"You are such a lovely child, Genevieve. Michael and I would love to think of you as an addition to our family." She melted away as Mum began to bellow within the house, shattering my almost dream-like stupor.

Had I dreamt all of that? Sometimes I wish Mum would shut up.

At school, I proved to be hopeless at most team sports. I found myself being hit in the face by flying balls because I wasn't concentrating or colliding with the other children because I wasn't good at judging distance. Twice I had broken windows because I was so badly co-ordinated that I had thrown the ball askew. PE lessons were very lonely times for me. I was the last child to be picked for a team, even after the fat child, and was usually sent back indoors as a punishment for day dreaming. Joe would offer to pick me first if he were made team captain but I had refused to let him take pity on me like that, explaining that there was something that I would soon discover I had a natural aptitude for.

In our last year of junior school we were introduced to ballet by a student Games teacher who had been assigned our class as a practice challenge. My flat feet ruled out a career as an elegant dancer but my natural flexibility didn't go unnoticed.

"Genevieve," she said as she marched us out of the changing room one day, "I think you should consider going to a gymnastics club or getting proper lessons. You're the right age to train your body to respond and I believe you'd enjoy it."

"Okay," I answered, "as long as my parents are alright with it."

"How will that help you concentrate, Genevieve?" Mum asked. "I want you to do better at school and go to Cambridge like Marcus, not spend your time jumping around."

"Gymnastics is not jumping around and I'm good at it, I think. Why won't you let me try? I'm rubbish at everything else. And my school marks are always top, you know that. You always compare me to the other two!" I grumbled, knowing very well that she wasn't listening to me.

Mum was not in any mood to listen to my bright idea, and Dad tended to come home after bedtime on a weekday, so tired that he just referred me back to her. So I took it upon myself to dip into my college fund and pay for my own gym tuition for the first month, to embarrass them into taking notice. It worked. Three times a week for the next two years, I got up at six in order to fit in an hour's pre-school gymnastics coaching at the local leisure centre.

Gymnastics did not have the impact on me that it did only because of the physical challenge. For the first time in my life, I actively socialised and made living friends other than Joe. There were three of them - Anna, Mary and Pascale. During my second coaching session, they sat with me while I was taking my shoes off. I had stiffened in response, suspecting I was in for a beating, as Philip and Daniella often cut off my escape route this way. Instead, Mary offered me some chopped apple and the rest of them smiled and shook my hand. It took another week to realise that they were not lulling me into a false sense of security before beating me up, but that they really did want to get to know me better. Making friends did not come naturally to me and the girls picked up on that very quickly, as children often do. They respected the fact that there were times when I would revert back to being a loner and needing to be silent. During these times they would chat amongst themselves, expressing their acceptance by sitting with me, sharing food and not directing conversation to me unless I invited it. I was content in their company, but even in the happiest of times I didn't feel that I truly belonged; the odd sensation of unfamiliarity always remained, crouching in my heart like a little toad.

Eventually I left gymnastics club when my parents could no longer afford to pay for it. It was the perfect time to leave; Mary had moved to a place called Hazelton, Pennsylvania, while Pascale's parents had taken her back to Paris and Anna had broken her foot, ending her gymnastics career. We wrote to one another on a regular basis though, keeping the four-way friendship alive for years afterwards.

I was fifteen when Anna suddenly died of a brain aneurysm. I knew it the moment she appeared in my room as I sat at my desk studying. She was only there for a split second, but the image of her smiling and radiant lingered in my heart for a long time afterwards. Two days after her death I received her last letter, wrapped around a tiny chunk of polished rose quartz. I recognised it as the one her grandmother had given her to make a pendant with.

"Genevieve, to love and protect you when I cannot," the letter said.

I have never cried for Anna. How could I, knowing the freedom, love and blissful existence she had when she passed over? *Now you're really living, my friend.*

The piece of rose quartz remained in a small pouch around my neck for the rest of my life.

The paved area outside the kitchen door was a great place to practise gymnastics. I loved doing cartwheels and back flips there. Depending on the time of day, I was joined by either John Graham or a few of the local labourers that Matthew employed. They found my gymnastic antics hugely entertaining and one of the younger farm hands would attempt handstands when I challenged him. Once or twice I even earned an unexpected round of applause from Matthew who had come to see what was distracting his workers.

"Trust you to bring a decent day's work to a standstill, Genevieve," he would say, in mock annoyance.

By contrast, John Graham was a quiet spectator who would join me on Sundays when the workers were at church or at home. Unlike the young men, he didn't attempt to join in, even when coaxed.

"Don't be frightened, John Graham. It's okay, I'll hold you."

"No, thank you. It's not because I'm frightened exactly… I don't want to fall ill again… or worse."

"Eh?"

"Gymnastics isn't what some would call acceptable behaviour."

"Who told you that?"

"I mustn't say here but I promise I'll tell you."

"Okay."

I had never seen John Graham acting furtively before and noticed that he sometimes glanced nervously at the dining room window. During times like these his mood would be low, so I would add an element of surprise to my routines by throwing a ball and catching it after a back flip or walking on my hands as I carried an empty watering can between my feet. It never failed to bring a smile to his face.

Whoever my audience was, I appreciated their attention and showed it by bowing dramatically at the end of every practice session and personally shaking each person's hand. What I didn't realise was that I had one extra audience member whose hand I never shook. Whether she was in the dining room, kitchen or Vanessa's room, my mother never missed a show. She never admitted to having watched me and never voiced her concerns to me or asked me any questions.

I only discovered all of this many years later when I read my personal file, which the prison psychiatrist had prepared.

Joe and I both did very well in our first year of secondary school. I managed to get top marks in our end of year exams in all subjects except Physics, which I failed only because I never agreed with the teacher's explanations. Joe was in every school sports team except netball (and that only because he wasn't a girl). It was the year he began to grow tall and I stopped growing. Eventually he would stop at six feet two, dwarfing my diminutive frame and making us look like the most mismatched couple at school.

As part of the deal that kept me with my peers, I had personal tutors to provide me with an extra academic challenge and, as a result, I began to enjoy school at times. In fact, the only day I detested was Tuesday, as science became the new bane of my life. I refused to dissect anything in Biology, managed to blow up everything I touched in Chemistry, and was usually kicked out of Physics for asking too many questions.

This year also saw the rediscovery of my paternal grandmother, ushering in a new era of self-discovery. Out of the blue I had received thirteenth birthday greetings from her, consisting of a very lavishly decorated calling card with her name, address and strict instructions not to bring "that bratty sister of yours". Three days later, as I walked towards the neat terrace off Watling Avenue where she lived, I realised that I couldn't recall anything about her apart from some fleeting images of high-heeled shoes and painted toenails at eye level. I looked again at the calling card just to be sure I'd got the correct house number.

Without a mental picture, how would I know I have the correct old lady?

I took a deep breath and stepped over the garden's threshold, half expecting a booby trap of some sort to finish me off. The gate was broken and the path to the front door was almost submerged in grass and naked dandelion heads. A bramble bush stood proud and wild to my right and I made a mental note to steal some of the blackberries for Joe in the summer if I came back. The shabby, peeling door swung open to reveal Grandma Kelly before I'd even reached for the doorbell. I was too taken aback to say more than "Hhh-h...h-h..." for the first few seconds, so we both stood in the doorway sizing each other up. My grandmother was strikingly beautiful for her seventy-plus years, which was what winded me for words.

She must have been ravishing in her youth, just like Vanessa is now. But I bet she was nicer to people.

She was statuesque, sharp-featured and breathtakingly elegant in her long, jade green silk dress. She wore a 1920s-style head-dress on her silver head and sucked on a long cigarette holder that was delicately balanced between long fingers. Eventually she broke the silence by asking:

"Why did you decide to develop a list when you walked to the door?"

"I tend to get my hair caught on bushes, that's why," I said, trying to flatten my mane a little.

"Would you like champagne or sherry?" she asked, with a grand flick of her elegant arm.

I didn't know what either tasted like so I asked for some hot water instead. It had been my choice of drink for some years now because of the comfort it brought to my stomach. Grandma Kelly looked absolutely disgusted as she turned on her heel and strode out of the lounge. I sat back on the rich, scarlet chaise longue and viewed my surroundings. My grandmother had been an actress in her heyday and the whole room was filled with theatre memorabilia from the 1920s and `30s. There were some pictures of her as a young woman with various screen personalities. On the mantelpiece stood photos of Dad and his brothers when they were children, but there was a glaring absence of adulthood and wedding photos and any reminders of my grandfather. Two minutes later I was presented with a pot of steaming hot chocolate and a china cup. I had to admit that it smelled delicious and I was glad Grandma Kelly had ignored my request.

"Why are you so small? Does your mother not feed you?" She was scrutinising me with beady eyes.

"Not sure. Vanessa and Marcus are tall but I don't seem to have caught up yet." I was not the least bit phased by her nosey scrutiny, being far too gone in chocolate-scented bliss to be offended by anything.

"Well, drink that. It won't make you any shorter. You're far too scrawny to be my grandchild the way you are".

Grandma Kelly tilted her chin upwards and gracefully turned her face away from me so that her perfect profile formed a cameo-like silhouette against the window behind her. I smiled to myself. She looked moody and sounded rude but the huge rose-pink bubble that emanated from her chest gave her away. Within seconds it had enveloped me and I knew instantly that I had a niche in my grandmother's life at least.

"I know what you are thinking. You've got the black hair from me and my mother," she said at last, softly and wistfully. Her eyes were focussed on a scene from many decades ago. "All my sons were robust and blond like my Kenneth." She sighed heavily. "Thirty-seven years ago and I still can't believe the bastard died on me."

"Why do you not have any photos of Dad, Grandpa and Uncles Laurie and Oliver grown up?" I asked very gently. I didn't want to upset her and I could already see a heavy cloud near her heart that corresponded with the slouch in her posture. It almost seemed to weigh down her chest, causing her spine to become concave.

"Oh, my life stopped when your grandfather died. I don't think I took many photos after that. It didn't seem worth it." She sighed again picking up the delicate bone china teacup in front of her and taking the tiniest sip of the drink inside. "Anyway, I was designed to be in front of the camera, not behind it."

Grandma Kelly winked at me and a small rose-coloured streamer emanated from between her breasts and made its way to my heart. It made me feel warm and I allowed myself to enjoy the sensation for as long as it lasted. It was not often that this happened and feeling it with my own grandmother was a wonderful treat.

"Where's that funny-looking dark boy you used to play with?"

"Oh, Joe?" I asked, trying desperately to hold back a fit of giggles. *Funny looking dark boy!* "He's got football practice today. I'll be meeting him later. Do you want to meet him too?"

"Not until he's your boyfriend," she said, winking wickedly at me and making me blush furiously.

We spent the next half hour or so listening to her pre-war record collection on a very well-maintained antique gramophone. She narrated stories from her childhood and described an old Edgware and Queensbury that had long since disappeared. The conversation soon made its way back to me:

"You may be wondering why I invited you here."

I nodded.

"Well, Genevieve, I'm not getting any younger and I would like to rest assured that there is some hope for all those left behind." She picked up on my uncertainty. "You may be confused but it's not something you will even begin to comprehend until you are much, much older and have experienced a lot more of life. I knew you were different from the moment I saw you as a new-born. You had the wise eyes of an old woman and I knew immediately that you would have a tough time comprehending human nature. I was exactly like you and so was my great aunt. I'm here to guide you, so never hesitate to come to me for anything, however small. Go home now and don't think too much about what I've just said. It will become clear in time. By the way…"

She reached out a long arm and plucked something small from behind one of the photo frames on the mantelpiece. It was a photograph of a chubby, happy baby, sitting by a window. The baby was gazing at something to the left of the photographer with an unmistakable look of wonderment and awe in its eyes. The light seeping in through the backdrop of net curtains formed a faint halo around the baby's head. I recognised the window as the one I was currently standing next to.

"I was the photographer," whispered Grandma Kelly, as she pushed my hair behind my shoulders, "and that baby is you." She took the photograph from my hands and put it in my pocket. "One day I will tell you what you were looking at when I took it."

As I walked out of the front door she readjusted the collar of my coat and looked very deeply into my eyes.

"Never forget who you are."

This statement was the greatest gift she ever gave me and it became the mantra that kept me alive during many years of trauma and imprisonment.

FIVE

Evelyn

*I'm actually losing it. My reality is so different
to everybody else's. Why?*

Making sure that nobody was around, I had set up the art room
for an experiment. I wanted to see what the energy pattern of an
egg would be if I shot it with my slingshot, making it ricochet off
the padded edge of the notice board before gently hitting a piece
of painted canvas on the adjacent wall. Then I intended to allow
the mess to dry and crack, hopefully resembling the glaze on an
old Renaissance fresco. To be extra considerate, I had even taped
toilet paper to the walls and nearby tables so that I could bundle it
up and throw it away when I was done. It started very well. I was
enthralled by the air splitting and eddying around the body of the
egg, as it flew towards the hard surface of the canvas.

Gosh, if only human movement could look like that. But then, eggs
don't have much colour because they haven't been born yet like we
have. There's a bit of life in them though. I wonder if I should inject
some dye next time or whether that would ruin the aerodynamics...

Hey, no two eggs move the same… if you look at them carefully…

"What on Earth are you doing, young lady?"

I jumped out of my skin and took a moment to collect the breath from lungs that had leaped up into my neck. Mrs Heathland stood towering above me, arms wrapped around her huge bosom as if to hold it in place. I watched as the colour rushed to her cheeks in anger. More acne erupted onto the surface of her skin before my very eyes. She was shouting something at me and expecting an answer but I couldn't hear her. I was far too enchanted by the sight of her tiny blood vessels beating under her skin. The energy rose from the surface of her face like steam.

Miss Ballentyne the Art teacher came in and offered to take over. Mrs Heathland turned to leave but not before throwing an empty toilet roll at me.

"What is all this, Genevieve?" asked Miss Ballentyne gently.

"I wanted to recreate the glazed effect, like da Vinci, and experiment with aerodynamics at the same time. The eggs light up like bulbs when they're moving. I protected everything from the mess, see." I pointed to the toilet paper, neatly positioned in strips side by side with not a bit of wall showing. She shook her head. "You don't like it, Miss Ballentyne?"

There was something about Miss Ballentyne that reminded me of my grandmother even though she was clearly a lot younger. She had also been a fashion model in her youth, but anorexia had ravaged her looks and ruined her career. There was a big, black spot near her heart. It beat when her heart did too, as though it were a conjoined twin.

"You're a very intelligent and artistic pupil, Genevieve, but this is absolute lunacy."

"It is? Why?" I didn't understand how gaining knowledge was considered madness.

"Look, I'm going to pretend to send you home as a punishment. I won't call your parents but I will call another responsible adult, okay? Any suggestions?"

My grandmother did not have a telephone as she preferred calling cards. Vanessa was at school too. Marcus was at home sleeping. His bar job only required evening shifts so he was free to attend interviews during the day. And, most importantly, he was unlikely to report this incident to Mum and Dad.

"My brother's an adult and he's home today. Not sure if he's responsible though."

Twenty minutes later, a bleary-eyed and crumpled Marcus arrived at school. He had a quick chat with Miss Ballentyne as I put on my coat. I noticed how similar his mannerisms were to Dad's and it made him appear strange. I had never really viewed my brother as a grown man before. We left school just as the lunch bell rang and had to weave our way through the crowd of kids that had spilled out of the classrooms and converged in the corridor. My older brother grabbed my hand in front of everybody, effectively ruining my credibility forever. I sighed when I saw some of my peers smirking at us.

"Do you reckon you can get Joe to fake a sickie so that I don't have to pick him up later?" Marcus asked.

"No chance, he's got football this afternoon."

Marcus had driven to school in the old Metro Mum and Dad had bought him for his twenty-first birthday. The inside had already begun to smell of cigarette smoke and fried chicken and there were stains all over the upholstery. I curled up in the passenger seat, allowing only the smallest surface area of my body to touch the seat. *There are only two layers of clothing between my arse and the dirty seat.* Marcus handed me a plastic bag to sit on but I politely refused it. I hated plastic more than dirt. At least dirt is natural.

"Marcus, am I going to have to bribe you to keep quiet about this?" He chuckled. For a moment he looked handsome.

"No, I'm curious to know why you did it though."

"I liked seeing the colours."

"What? I don't get you." He looked at me and drummed the steering wheel for a moment like Dad did when he was thinking. I felt obliged to continue.

"The colours of the egg as it moves - it cuts through the other colours around it, merging them at the edges." Nothing. Marcus stopped drumming and stared at me. Behind us a car honked but Marcus did nothing.

"What colour is air, Genevieve?"

"It depends on what the atmosphere is like and how the energy is moving. I can't explain very well."

"Hold on, hold on, you can't see air. It just exists."

"Says who?"

"It's an accepted fact. Scientific fact."

"Science doesn't decide what I see."

"Space is air. It's black because of an absence of light, of energy."

"I don't think so and that's what matters to me."

"Fine! Ravi's a scientist and he's coming over," said Marcus, as he pulled into the driveway and crushed one of mum's hydrangeas. "We'll see what he says."

"Go ahead. It won't change anything for me, Marcus."

As if on cue, Ravi appeared from around the fence. Marcus and I were still arguing in the car as he approached and we both jumped when he tapped on the window. Marcus took ages to find the keys to the front door. He was wearing combat trousers with several pockets in them and was too tired to function properly. Finally, he fished them out of the pocket on his left thigh, dropping them twice before they reached the keyhole. In the meantime, I studied Ravi. Unlike the rest of the female species, my interest in Ravi was purely academic. He reminded me of Joe sometimes and that was all I wished to see in him.

"Ravi, why are you spending the afternoon with Marcus?" I asked.

"Why shouldn't I?"

"Because he's boring."

"He's also graduated from Cambridge, which is where I wish to go."

Ravi was filling in something called an UCCA form and another form especially for Cambridge University. Until last year, I had only ever heard of Kings College, Oxford and Cambridge. The former was where Archbishop Desmond Tutu studied for his postgraduate degree. It was also where Marcus had originally wanted to go but he'd ended up going to Cambridge due to parental pressure and exceptional A Level grades. Lately, I became aware of Bristol University but only because I'd been forced to watch University Challenge when Marcus was at home. I ran upstairs, changed my egg-stained clothes and entered the kitchen just in time for a cup of tea.

"Hey Ravi, Genevieve reckons you can see space."

"So?"

"She sees air. Is that not weird?"

"Not for a twelve year old," said Ravi, looking a little confused.

"I'm thirteen now," I said, not bothering to hide my annoyance.

"Why are you taking her side?" asked Marcus, a little irritated by Ravi's apparent indifference.

"I'm not. Why are you trying to humiliate her? You're twenty-one. Why do you care what she thinks?" he said.

"Because she gets sent home from school for it."

Ravi looked at me enquiringly. I couldn't be bothered to give him a full explanation so I gave him a partial one.

"I wanted to conduct a Physics and Art experiment at the same time so I shot eggs at a canvas via the frame of the notice board."

"Cool. What happened?" he asked. I could tell he was genuinely intrigued.

"I got caught."

"No, I mean what was the effect?"

"Oh, I didn't get that far. It was supposed to glaze over like a Renaissance painting." I began to feel like my head was being probed and the air around me started to change and become a bit pinker. Ravi smiled at me and his face momentarily morphed into Joe's. My stomach flipped and I began to feel uncomfortable. "Well, gentlemen, I'm going upstairs to get my homework done."

"Bye, Genevieve," said Ravi. "That sweater's nice, by the way, brings out the colour of your eyes."

I ran upstairs feeling sick. But it was not Marcus' fault this time.

As the leaves rotted and eventually disappeared from the ground, I noticed a definite change in the health and appearance of little John Graham. Gone was the endless enthusiasm, boundless energy and eternally flushed cheeks. In their place came dull eyes, listlessness and pallor. More alarming still was the deep, hacking cough that consumed his tiny frame and inhabited his little lungs. It had no intention of abating even to the slightest degree. Instead it squatted in his air passages and struck with full force every time he exerted himself. The sight of his blue face after a coughing fit terrified me and I prayed that each particular episode would not bring up blood or bits of lung. During those times when he gasped for even half a breath and clutch his shirt in pain, I would have done anything to swap places with him and ease his burden.

I'm stronger than him and yet I can only watch him suffer, I thought, as he simultaneously coughed and yelped in pain. *Our Father, who art in Heaven, hallowed be Thy name. Are you even there?* Neither inspiration, nor sign, nor gut feeling came to the rescue. *Please God. Help my friend. I'll behave forever, I promise.* It was no use. God wasn't listening.

Around the same time, John Graham began to mention an addition to the Davis family. I didn't meet Evelyn Bingham until after

Christmas, but the way John Graham shuddered whenever he spoke of her made me realise that not making her acquaintance was a good thing. Apparently, she was Michael Davis' half-sister from Ireland, a spinster who was as bitter and vile as an unripe lemon. She made a sport out of being cruel and often beat John Graham as he lay in his sick bed. I vowed to get revenge the day he showed me the bright red welts across his forearms from her weapon of choice, a long strip of leather that she carried tucked into the apron she wore, along with the keys to all the locks in the house and a tiny, black Bible. We sat by the small fireplace in John Graham's room, stoking the already roaring blaze. John Graham shivered in the heat of the contained inferno and pulled the blanket tighter around his shoulders. He coughed pathetically and gazed at me sadly.

"Promise me you'll never let anybody punish you like this," he said with the tiniest voice.

"I promise," I replied and took him, all feverish and exhausted, into my arms. It dawned on me then that a part of the reason John Graham had passed away so young was that he had simply given up.

My first encounter with Evelyn Bingham was the day I discovered what true terror was. I had just come home from school and was looking forward to throwing down my dead-weight school bag and feeling the sweet relief of shaking my aching arms. But there was a strange, unnerving smell emanating from my room and the crackle of static filled my ears once again. The smell turned into a stench as I ascended the stairs and hit me in the chest and stomach, making me feel a weird queasiness that overpowered my body and clouded my judgement. I stopped for a second and leaned against the wall to take stock of what was happening. The bedroom door was ajar but the gap was not sufficient for me to see inside. Not sure what to do, I braced myself, took a deep stink-filled breath and yanked the door open briskly. Evelyn Bingham swung around to face me, arm raised, belt in hand, ready to strike. She was horrible to look at. There was a huge, black cloud around her and I could just about make out her severe features and tight topknot through it. Her eyes were piercing and filled with hatred.

John Graham was cowering in his bed with his arms in the air, anticipating the next blow. The funny smell was coming from him, but not because he had pooed himself in fright; it was a different smell, more physical than merely olfactory and far too pungent to be excrement. *I can smell his fear…*

Evelyn and I stood glaring at one another as my terror swiftly turned to rage. I was the only protection John Graham had and I was not about to waste the opportunity I now had of telling Evelyn what I thought of her.

"You dumb bitch!" I hissed, launching my school bag at her.

The three of us watched it fly straight through her and land with a thump by the window. Her cloud became blacker and thicker.

Think, Genevieve, think!

I picked up a piece of coal from the fireplace and threw it at her. It hit her square in the face and I caught her pursing her lips just before lunging at me, an almighty roar working its way up from her belly and out of her mouth making her appear inhuman for a moment. I knew I couldn't leave John Graham at her mercy but he was nowhere in sight. Had he escaped? I managed to duck in the split second that the belt descended and hit the patch of wall behind where my head had been. As I turned to flee, I caught a glimpse of that patch of wall. The blow had dislodged a sliver of plaster.

I did not stop running until I reached the kitchen. My heart was drumming a dead-beat rhythm against my ribs, rattling my torso uncontrollably. Perspiration seeped through every pore of my body. Where was my mother? My mind wandered back to the piece of coal. *I know how to play you at your own game, Evelyn…*

Vanessa breezed in and put the kettle on. I had never been so relieved to see her.

"You look like shit," she said nonchalantly, without even looking up.

Okay Genevieve, she may not provide the same level of security as Mum but she's bad-tempered and a veteran of school cat fights.

With this in mind I made my way up the stairs again. My heart was pounding so furiously that I was convinced Evelyn would hear it and launch a pre-emptive strike. But the thought of her lashing at John Graham with her leather strap rekindled my fury and propelled me towards the bedroom door.

I stood in the doorway, forlornly surveying my bedroom. It was quiet, as it should be. The books were strewn over my desk, as they should be. Several items of clothing were draped over the back of my chair, as they should be. The cuddly toys lined up against the wall were staring back at me, as they should be. I plonked myself down on the end of the bed and sighed, but not with relief. My rage gave way to concern for John Graham's safety.

Gradually our new house began to give away clues about its character, and it was far from pleasant. Life within its sinister walls taught me a new spectrum of negative emotions I hadn't experienced before. Coming home from school was the worst time of day; when it should have filled me with relief, it drummed up an acute feeling of dread that rose up from the pit of my skinny abdomen. As soon as I set foot across the threshold, I was swallowed up by an atmosphere of oppression, fear and death - unnatural death. Walking up the stairs towards my bedroom was frightening; I always had the feeling that I was being followed and yet, when I turned around, the hallway would be clear. I often walked up and down the hall and stairs, running my fingers along the walls, trying to read the indentations and undulations.

Taking a shower would set off terrible episodes of paranoia as I imagined forms of strange people materialising in the mist, peering through the steamed up glass as I bathed. Those same forms would stand by my bed as I tried in vain to sleep, lying in wait as I cowered under the duvet and blocked my ears to the sound of alien breathing.

Oh my god, Vanessa's right, I'm going mad. I'm actually losing it. And yet this all seems real to me. My reality is so different to every-body else's. Why?

My journey towards the karate class should have taken only fifteen minutes on foot, twenty at the most. However, my aversion to the far side of Honeypot Lane meant that it became a forty-five minute excursion through various avenues, lanes and crescents. For five long years I wondered why walking along that seemingly harmless pavement of Honeypot Lane should invoke a tidal wave of nausea in my unsuspecting belly. There were numerous occasions when I would vomit suddenly in the street, whispering weak apologies to passers-by between retches. Eventually I gave up fighting fate and found a different route. I was fourteen when Honeypot Lane and its environs gave me my explanation. Joe and I were making our way towards Kingsbury Park to play Frisbee when I began to get the familiar leaden feeling in my legs. Technically we had not yet set foot on Honeypot Lane but I knew from experience that the moment I did, the heavy, sick feeling would travel upwards to my stomach and fester for a while before bursting forth at its chosen point along the road. I stopped at the tiny bridge over the brook to catch my breath. Joe waited patiently and threw twigs in the water to pass the time.

As I stared into the distance, 1993 faded away and I was left standing in a field by a much larger body of water. In front of me and stretching as far as the eye could see was the aftermath of a battle. The ground was littered with splayed and dismembered bodies of men, horses and even cattle. In the distance, two men in Roman armour were walking amongst the bodies, studying them and occasionally sticking a sword into one. Afterwards a pack of dogs obediently standing by would tear the body up, eliminating any chance of survival.

I heard pitiful sobbing behind me and turned round. A withered old man was staring beyond me at the bloody ground, his hands tightly gripping the part of his chest that held his heart. The weight of his pain was evident in his tortured eyes and the sight of him left an imprint on my memory forever. He spluttered something in a Latinate language and pointed to a chunk of meat lying on the blood-soaked grass nearby. I understood what he meant. That had been his son.

I knelt by the pool of blood and gore and picked a string of glass beads from the dead grey hand resting there. With cupped hands I offered them back to the old man but, rather than take them, he put his hands on my shoulders, looked deeply into my soul and smiled through his pain, lifting the weight in an instant.

"My only son died before having the chance to make his mark in the world and he remained where he died until he became part of the earth. Every day for eternity I have come here to pray for an end to my sorrow. Now I know that the future will know him, I can finally rest in peace." I watched as he buried the beads in a nearby patch of marshland that I recognised. "Little one, these are here for you. Thank you for bringing me peace."

Nearly two millennia later, I dug some of them up and used them as a rosary.

After eight nights of non-stop digging, I still hadn't found them. Joe was standing next to me, shining a torch into the ever-deepening pit and yawning. Even though it had been a hot summer by English standards, Stanmore marshes remained damp, which had made

sieving the freshly dug ground impossible. Therefore I was forced to poke and prod every sod of earth to check for the beads before hurling it over my shoulder. Joe managed to dodge all of them except one.

"Hey, watch it!"

"Sod's law, Joe. That's sod's law."

At least Mum won't be short of a kitchen sieve. My gut feeling tells me they're here, so where are they?

At around 2 a.m. on the ninth night I finally struck beads. They were so dirty that I very nearly mistook them for pebbles, but some feeling told me to take a closer look and I was thankful I did. The thin leather strap that held them together had long since rotted away but all twenty-seven beads were present in my muddy palms, albeit misshapen and covered in dirt. Some of them disintegrated as I scraped the mud off but the majority remained whole. I was so pleased.

"What are we doing here?" Joe asked as I gyrated with delight. "Are you ever going to tell me?"

"I lost something when I fainted here the other day." Joe and I had not got to play Frisbee as I had vomited, fainted and been carried home.

"Genevieve, you fainted on the other side of the road." It was true. I had.

"Actually, my grandmother buried these as a child and I wanted to surprise her by finding them and returning them."

Joe would believe that, he thought Grandma Kelly was mad anyway. Luckily, he just rolled his eyes and started kicking the mounds of disturbed earth back into their original resting places.

I had been plagued by minor chest infections as a child but by the time I reached my mid-teens it had graduated to seasonal bronchitis. It was the only time my paternal grandmother would come to our house, on the pretext of looking after me while Mum and Dad went to work. During the first few days when my fever was at its peak and my chest felt as though it were on fire, she would make me mulled wine and entertain me with stories from her youth until I passed out in a drunken stupor. Grandma Kelly loathed antibiotics.

"If you have a weak digestion, which you do, they only weaken it further. We didn't have this rubbish in my day and I'm in better health than you." She had a point there.

For some unknown reason, Grandma Kelly did not have much to say to Dad or Mum and vice versa. I was too shy to ask directly but the change in her whenever one of them was around was unbelievable. The only way I can describe it is that I could sense an invisible wall go up around her like a huge, almost solid barrier, and within that she would cocoon herself in dark pink, eddying clouds. The barrier was so intense and impenetrable that I had difficulty making out any of her features. She looked like a big, swirling egg. She would deconstruct the fortress whenever they left and turn her attention to me with a bittersweet smile. Sometimes she gave me a hug. I did not like to be touched anymore and never opened up to a hug from anyone, but Grandma Kelly was the exception.

Her subliminal treatment of Vanessa was even worse. In fact, it was so underhand and cheeky that the odd giggle would escape me every now and again. The barrier would remain down but Grandma used the opportunity to throw little energy darts at Vanessa who did not appear to feel them physically but would accuse Grandma of bugging her. Poor Vanessa, she didn't understand why her own grandmother irritated her just by sitting in the same room, minding her own business.

Observing Grandma Kelly during times like these was a real treat. She was very unusual in the most wonderful way any mortal could hope to be, and men still stopped to admire her as she floated past in her heels and faux-fur stole (she never wore an ordinary coat). Eveningwear was her choice of everyday wear whatever the weather and her hair was always immaculately coiffed.

I watched her very closely one day when I was feeling particularly ill. She sat at the end of the sofa by my feet, embroidering something silk. Her long fingers gently pushed, teased and tugged as she stared at a spot a little to the left of the television. Every now and again her long, mascara-coated lashes quivered and a smile spread slowly across her face. She was thinking about an event that had taken place in her youth.

A tall, blond boy was asking her to dance with him but she refused, saying she had to go home. She was young – maybe a few years older than I am now – and she wore a gold hair band with a little feather in it. The feather was blown away by a sudden gust of wind but the blond boy chased after it and caught it. Grandma clapped with joy and allowed him to walk her home. On the way she confessed that she would have loved to have danced with him, but had been frightened of looking like a rooster on the dance floor as her limbs were so long and thin. The boy, Kenneth, spent the next twenty years teaching her how to dance.

My head jerked back when I realised that I was watching her thoughts. Or was I? Maybe I was delirious with fever or simply overtired. I closed my eyes and pretended to sleep, leaving Grandma Kelly to the privacy of her own imagination.

I was twelve years old when Vanessa was discovered by a modelling agent in the Brent Cross Shopping Centre. Mum was dragging us from shop to shop, pushing us in front of the full-length mirrors in turn and scrutinising the colour, size and practicality of each coat that she held against us. For the last couple of years, Vanessa had proved a nightmare to shop for as she had long since outgrown teenage clothes and the choices in adult sizes were not to her taste. This was often the basis of public rows between Vanessa and Mum that I wandered away from, pretending to be totally separate from them.

Vanessa first noticed the woman looking her up and down approvingly in Top Shop. After a few minutes Vanessa stomped towards her wearing her practised mask of bad attitude and aggression.

"What you looking at, lady pervert?" she asked, loud enough for other shoppers in the vicinity to stop what they were doing and look up at her. I disappeared into the jeans rail and watched. Mum walked towards Vanessa and stood next to her as if rooted to the spot. There was a shield of pink around her and it extended to include Vanessa. My head began to hurt and I was struggling to breathe deeply. The atmosphere has become oppressive and hostile. Mum looked a little perplexed but I knew from experience and her stance that she was more than ready to defend her daughter.

"What's going on?" she asked in an authoritative manner, her back straightened to full height. Together the three of them could have been trees in a forest to me. *Dad and Marcus are tall too. I'm adopted for sure, but that's okay.*

"I was wondering if your daughter has ever thought about modelling, that's all," she said coolly, as she handed Mum her card. I noticed that she held the card between her index and middle fingers and not with her thumb. Her nails were shiny and long, looking odd at the end of her wrinkly and dehydrated hands. I could not be sure how old she was but she looked like a used tea bag, dull and dry. She held her head back haughtily in order to look at Vanessa down the length of her pinched nose. There was something about her that made me uneasy. The word 'vulture' came to mind as I watched her bird-like eyes flit from one face to another. She must have spotted some more prey because then she tick-tocked off in her stilettos, her eyes fixed on a new target.

I'll bet she has some kind of built-in radar.

She turned back to look at us and I gulped.

Did she hear what I thought just then?

Mum would always ensure that she was free to accompany Vanessa to her modelling shoots, cutting back on the hours she worked which meant that Dad often worked overtime. I became a latchkey child but didn't resent it in the slightest. On the contrary, I found that being alone for a couple of hours a day proved very productive. I finished my homework in half the normal time and then strolled to Canons Park to see Matthew and his horses. The flipside was that I often ended up dwelling on any negative situations that had occurred during the day. I would analyse, debate and re-analyse, ending up bewildered and utterly confused about how and where I fitted in. I eventually internalised my bewilderment by literally swallowing it down with massive gulps of air. The grey, heavy energy would then settle around my tummy, making it gurgle in rebellion. If I ignored it, my abdomen would begin to twist and cramp, causing me pain; rubbing it only pushed the internalised emotion to another place causing a similar pain.

How can I be so much closer to the trees and animals than fellow human beings? I just don't understand how they think or why they do what they do. I mean, what is rage or hatred or even words? Yes, what are words? They're superfluous. If we only noticed each other's proper forms and colours, there would be far less misunderstandings. One day, maybe words will be redundant. Right, tree?

I would rest against the sturdy trunk and end up deciding that I was really an alien sent to Earth to observe the human race and take notes on mankind. The absurdity of this would make me inwardly chuckle and bring me back to the moment.

God, how I hate it here!

Over the course of that winter I noticed a definite change in my sister. Physically she appeared more groomed, with neater eyebrows and glossier hair, but the real change was in what surrounded her. For a while now I'd been seeing conical shapes around people, small vortices that occurred at regular intervals up and down the central part of the person's body. Sometimes if I blinked hard they would disappear and I would really have to concentrate to see them again. I could not be sure but they seemed to 'feed' the bubble, or at least metabolise whatever was in it, a bit like eating, digesting and then pooing. For example, when Mum became angry a dark red cloud would brew up around her chest cone. It would then travel through the cone to her body where, upon absorption, she would shout or throw something. With the action, the dark red cloud would shoot out to the person she shouted at and be sucked into their system via one of their cones and they would become upset.

Vanessa's conical vortices began to change in size and shape around the time her attitude began to alter. The most sudden change was in the cone that came out of her privates and ended up near the ground. It became huge and open and simultaneously Vanessa became arrogant and more vain. The cones behind her grew and the ones in front shrank to compensate. Two on her head completely closed and the one behind her head became skewed. Vanessa lost her belief in God and her concern for other people - everything began to revolve around money, looks and all that they could buy.

Her success as a model came at exactly the right time for the family though. The hefty mortgage and interest rates gave Mum furrowed lines on her forehead and turned Dad's hair grey. Recession meant nothing to me at the time but my parents' invisible worries meant a lot. They spent longer with the bills and calculator, Mum was constantly worried about the cost of this and that and would snap at the slightest provocation and Dad would be seen staring into space at the dinner table. I hadn't noticed until then that we had not been to France for two years and had forgone school trips, professional haircuts and family outings for quite a while. Lazy Marcus also now had two jobs, as a catalogue model and a barman, to pay his own way through postgraduate studies. But my sister grew increasingly resentful of having to hand over a percentage of her earnings, which led to huge and prolonged arguments. During these, Vanessa would threaten to leave home as soon as was legal and refuse to stay on at school beyond her GCSEs. I became the target of a lot of her projected anger and found myself dodging cutlery, books and shoes on a regular basis.

"Stop staring at me, you fucking freak!" she would scream.

I didn't mean to stare at her. The angry and restless clouds around her were what interested me. Otherwise she didn't register in my limited and selective attention span. Vanessa eventually did leave, the day after obtaining her A Level results. In her wake she left a rotten pot-pourri of bad feelings - relief, loss, anger, abandonment, sadness and worry. Mum continued as though nothing had happened and Dad was upset, not because Vanessa had gone but because she'd moved in with her thirty-seven year old boyfriend; I would sit by the window of her old bedroom and... just sit. There was no strong emotion attached to Vanessa's departure for me, other than relief and possibly the faint awareness of a void.

I wonder when Vanessa will become a stranger to me. Did I ever really feel otherwise?

John Graham's mood would improve during November each year. For a limited time his cheeks would flush and his blue eyes would sparkle behind his glasses. The stomachs of Michael and Margaret would calm down and resume normal digestion. These phenomena coincided with Evelyn Bingham's annual trip back to Ireland around the time of her birthday. It was part of the deal she had with her half-brother. Evelyn would keep order in the home and Michael would pay for her passage back to Ireland for the month. Many times I heard Michael and Margaret discussing Evelyn. Margaret had her reservations, suspecting that her health and her husband's had begun to deteriorate since Evelyn's arrival. But Michael always chose to give his half-sister the benefit of the doubt.

"My darling," he would say tenderly, "she's the only family I have left other than you and our children. We need her here. Who will look after John?"

"But he's frightened of her, Michael. Have you not seen the change in him?"

"He's just delicate at the moment and he frightens easily. It will be alright."

Evelyn Bingham was the first person I had ever been afraid of and I wanted to face my fear head-to-head. Maybe I was just being youthfully impetuous but the fear had given birth to a dogged determination to get to the bottom of the ominous gut feeling she evoked. I was determined to expose her, for my own sake if not that of John Graham. He didn't have to form the exact words to tell me what he was going through; instinct told me that every moment he remained in the house beyond his death was a cry for help. How many years must he have waited to be noticed? There was a reason why he had not moved on and Evelyn Bingham was the key, of that I was certain.

She had lived in the attic room that Marcus slept in when he stayed over. I rarely ventured up there for obvious reasons. As soon as the door creaked open, it was like stepping into another space and time. The room was a few degrees colder than the rest of the house even though it was high up and well insulated. The air was thick with alien smells that I could not place in the present. Strange ideas of potions, medications and concoctions would pop into my head and I knew they were not mine. Yet for four long months I could find no tangible trace of Evelyn Bingham anywhere in the room.

Eventually it happened. I walked into Evelyn's room one cold day in February. Its austerity shocked me. I may as well have been standing in a convent room. There were very little personal objects in the room and absolutely no colour bar the entire spectrum of grey. The mattress from the bed had been removed and was leaning against the wall. A thick, grey blanket had been neatly tucked over the bare cot and another had been folded to form a pillow. A stone crucifix lay on the only non-grey item of furniture in the room, a wooden bedside table. Underneath the table, peeping out from under a greyish-white flannel was a metal basin, dented and abused. I imagined Evelyn hurling it at John Graham and my breath stopped momentarily. I closed my eyes and turned away from the basin, squeezing my eyeballs until they hurt. When I opened them again I found myself facing a queer-looking box-like object hidden beneath a large grey blanket. Assuming the cleanliness of the blanket to mean that it was regularly swept off to reveal the object underneath, I decided to venture a guess as to what it could be.

A coffin? Wrong shape. A wardrobe? Too small. A clock? Too squat.

I held my breath and lifted the edge of the blanket a few inches.

Curiosity killed the cat, I heard my mother's voice inside my head. *Maybe so, but I could be hit by a bus tomorrow and at least this way I will know...*

I lifted the blanket still further until I was able to fold it back over itself. How strange. A locked display cabinet full of tiny jars and bottles was hidden underneath it. I tried jiggling the door but it was locked tightly and there was no handle to pull on. There was nothing nearby that I could attempt to pick it with; the room was bare.

A noise outside startled me. I realised that somebody was ascending the stairs and I was trapped. There was not even anywhere to hide and the tiny window was sealed shut with years of dirt and dust.

I can feign ignorance. Make it look like I got lost. What choice do I have?

As I pulled the grey blanket down, my gaze fell for a split second onto a large labelled bottle in that cabinet.

ARSE.

Eh?

I repositioned the blanket in the nick of time.

"Why are you up here, Tiger? And why do you look so puzzled?" asked Dad, panting a little from the exertion of ascending the steep flight. I blinked and sighed with relief, wiping away the tiny beads of perspiration on my upper lip and forehead. *That was so close.*

"Just looking for the encyclopaedia."

"Have you seen my toolbox?" Dad said, safe in his own world where sense ruled.

"It's in the shed."

A few weeks later, Evelyn Bingham exacted her revenge upon me. Suspicion that she had somehow known of my snooping had not even entered my mind. How could she have found out? I had not taken anything away nor moved nor disturbed anything significantly. I was fastidious and meticulous in my criminal antics and I respected Evelyn as a formidable enemy. I would never have insulted her intelligence by being sloppy. Since that day I hadn't had an opportunity to discuss my detective work with John Graham and I certainly hadn't breathed a word to anybody else for fear of undermining my own sanity. Maybe she truly was the devil who existed in the shadows and crevices of that god-forsaken house. Who could I tell?

I had just put the laundry basket down by the bathroom door at the top of the stairs when her rage sent me hurtling down them to the cavernous silence of the hallway below. The moment I straightened my back again two hands made contact with it and the force was so great that I didn't land until the third to last step, hitting my head on the banister and sending me away with the stars. I landed facing the top of the staircase. Evelyn stood like death incarnate, silhouetted against the flashing lights in my bruised skull.

Touché, Evelyn, job well done.

With a swish of her grey monotone skirt she disappeared around the banister leaving me reeling from the screaming in my head.

God did not bless me with unconsciousness this time and I was home alone. I lay there as the sun set, allowing rectangles of light from outside to filter through the glass panes in the door and creep along the floor. I must have tried peeling myself off the carpet half a dozen times but the pain sent every small effort back to the very beginning again. The tears seeping from my eyes and running down the sides of my face began to pool in my ears and turn my hair soggy. Had I been in less pain and feeling less insulted I would have become irritated with the situation. But instead it drove me mad and I laughed like a fool for a while until my head throbbed violently.

After what seemed like an eternity, the keyhole rattled and somebody came home.

"Oh, you are fucking joking," said an inconvenienced Vanessa. I had never been so delighted to see her frowning face bending over me as she jammed the 9 key down three times.

Miraculously, no bones had been broken and there was no sign of concussion. I did have a bruised head and most of my joints and limbs were a patchwork of black and blue and red and purple. These were my battle wounds. Evelyn Bingham had become an intrinsic part of the enormous personal war that would consume the remaining eighteen years of this life.

SIX

Family

Dad, is there any remote possibility
that I was swapped at birth?

"Why won't you tell me what's going on in your mind? I am your mother."

I was so sick of this conversation. Most evenings I would go downstairs to the kitchen for my bedtime snack and find my mother sitting alone at the dining table waiting for me. It never varied. She would sit with a half-filled cup of cold coffee in front of her, staring at the wall opposite and twisting the wedding ring round and round on her finger. I felt like her prey. When I walked past her she would grab my arm without looking up and firmly steer me to sit in front of her. Then the questions would begin.

"Are you still being bullied?"

"Why won't you talk to me?"

"Why won't you talk to your father?"

"Would you prefer to talk to Vanessa? She's your age."

"What's wrong with you?"

113

"Are you even aware that you're behaving strangely?"

Sometimes her questions would cause me to laugh out loud, which would lead to her changing tactics. The questions would become orders and statements.

"Genevieve, you must realise that there's help if you need it."

"Only you can help yourself."

"Go to church more often. It will give you mental peace, really calm your mind."

"Genevieve, *we* love you but people out in the world don't. People talk."

At first I would answer her questions, tell her what I thought she wanted to hear. It began to dawn on me that this was fruitless and she had never heard - would never hear - a word I said. The vagueness in her eyes and the creases in the centre of her forehead were always present. There was an enormous gulf between us and, as cruel as it may sound, I preferred it that way. I now felt smothered by my mother's presence in a way that I could not understand. There was something about her that made me feel as though I were being bulldozed every time we came into contact with one another. Her energies were strong and vital and, while she was capable of the deepest affection and selflessness, she invisibly pushed me aside whenever I came near. Although I never felt rejected by her, I was aware that we would always exist on parallel lines, never to meet at any wavelength of mutual comprehension. We rarely fought because of this, certainly not in the way that she did with Vanessa or even Dad. I hated confrontation anyway but I was very fearful of my mother's energies engulfing me and extinguishing my own weak existence through their own sheer force. Maybe she was subconsciously aware of this too and sought to preserve me by internalising her anger and replacing it with a show of worry instead. Whatever the reason, I felt terribly guilty whenever she was sat at the dining table with her cold coffee, millions of miles away.

Our 'discussion' would end abruptly when she got up to do

something. Usually it was to wash her cup before she went upstairs to talk to Dad or make me something to eat. I would watch her as she put the mask on. One minute she would be creased with concern, the next she would jump up with a smile so big it was scary and rummage in the fridge, chirping about something random as she did so.

"Come Genevieve, what shall I make for you? Something healthy to make you grow." It astounded me that after all these years she still did not realise that I was not going to get much bigger, however much I ate. I wonder if she ever really noticed *me* at all.

There were times when she would force Dad to do the dirty work and talk to me. I could tell when she had nagged him into complying. He would knock on my door or cough lightly to get my attention. Then he would stand in plain view, looking down at the floor as he adjusted the belt of his jeans and then re-adjusted it back again. Dad was as transparent as glass and it sometimes made me laugh. Unlike Mum, he put me at my ease, leaving an open ground on which we could talk as equals. Talking to my Dad was a good way of learning about my mother from a new perspective.

"Well... er, Gen... er... Tiger, sorry. We need to talk about... er... how you're getting on."

"Did Mum put you up to this?"

"No... I mean... she cares about you, that's all. Yes, yes she did. But only because she cares, mind."

"I don't mind talking but there's not much to talk about. You can ask me if I'm mad, but I'll always say no because I'm not, according to me."

"It's not about your sanity, Tiger."

"Well, I'm not having sex or smoking so what else could it be about?"

Dad sighed. He had no idea how to deal with women even after nearly thirty years of marriage to one and bringing up two. At this point he would rub his eyebrows and plonk himself down on the settee. It creaked in complaint.

"Dad, I'm fine. There's nothing to worry about. I just hate noise."

"I know that but she doesn't, does she?" he would say. "All girls are supposed to be like Vanessa and become hormonal over burnt toast and have marathon sessions on the `phone with friends they'll see an hour later. I don't understand it but it makes perfect sense apparently."

"Is she annoyed with me then?"

"No, Tiger. I think she's just jealous."

"Of whom?"

"My mother."

"Why?"

"You talk to her, that's why."

"Because she listens … Mum gets jealous?"

I had never imagined that my mother would ever be jealous of anything. I had certainly never seen her jealous. It made sense on the surface but that was all. I laughed. Dad joined me.

A few minutes later Mum walked in with a big scowl on her face. There had been no tell-tale floorboard creaks to suggest that she'd been eavesdropping this time. My mother often eavesdropped, especially when Vanessa was on the `phone, so I wasn't surprised at all. She was obviously in a bad mood and made a point of throwing cushions into place while Dad was still sitting on the sofa. As he put them aside she picked them up and threw them back, aiming at his torso. Dad let the cushions bounce off him and sighed again.

"What have I done now, Eloise?"

I began to feel squeezed against the back of the chair I was sitting on.

"Genevieve, go upstairs now," Mum ordered.

I tried but felt rooted to the spot by an invisible pressure. This irritated Mum even more.

"I wanted you to speak to her, not turn it into a joke! You always do that! You never take anything seriously!" she screeched.

I managed to stand up and held on to the chair while I straightened my back. All around me there was thick ooze. I could not breathe or open my eyes and I wanted to get outside so desperately. Luckily I was near the door.

"We were talking, just like we always do. There's nothing wrong with laughing with your daughter. Maybe if you did once in a while..."

I felt Mum push past me and the door slammed.

Suddenly, the atmosphere cleared. There were small stationary wisps of spent anger floating around but they were benign and I didn't feel them.

My Mum is jealous of my relationship with my Dad? Why? I don't understand jealousy. Must be hormonal like Dad mentioned. I'll probably be like that soon.

Matthew and I sat on the fallen branch of an enormous tree on the outskirts of the duke's estate. For the last hour or so I had sat frozen, wide-eyed, lapping up the passionate words that had been expertly woven together by Matthew to make up a spoken tapestry chronicling the duke's life. I enjoyed watching his normally deadpan face come to life. It was rare for his mouth, rather than his eyes, to do most of the communicating. We had started swapping stories instead of the horse riding lessons that Matthew had promised once. I had grown only two and a half inches since then and had not put on much weight either. He had offered to get a pony to teach me on but I had refused; it was either horse riding or nothing.

"You may shoot up when you're sixteen," Matthew said, to make me feel better. When he realised that it didn't bother me in the slightest he would add, "but I doubt it. You can always tell how tall a person will grow by the size of their hands. Yours are tiny. Can't measure horses with those." I looked down at my hands and turned them over, examining them while he continued. "You weren't born to muck out stables and do my kind of work. You're a lady and don't you forget that."

From then on I noticed a person's hands before anything else, even clothes and eyes.

Matthew had taken me for a long walk around the periphery of the duke's estate. For the most part we walked in silence. Every now and again he stopped and pointed to something of interest and explained its significance. In between he tore off a large mouthful of the pasty he was holding and chewed it violently. He had used to bring a smaller one for me but gave up when he realised that he would invariably end up having to eat it himself. Matthew did not understand vegetarianism and blamed it for my lack of stature.

"It was in jest when I said it would put hair on your chest and chin, Genevieve."

"I know."

"Do you not want to learn to ride the horses?"

"Not if it means eating meat."

"You're stubborn."

"I know."

However, he respected my eating habits and started bringing me bread with apple jam or herb butter instead.

"Here, eat this. If you were my child I'd let you starve."

"I know."

We spent the rest of the day walking in silence. It was not only because Matthew was so frugal with words. We shared a profound respect for nature and the environment. There was no need to express that to one another, it was apparent. Often the beauty of our bond was that we could communicate through the contented silences that formed the foundation of our odd friendship. When

the first whispers of twilight began to veil the sky, Matthew walked me back to Whitchurch.

"Genevieve, about that dark boy," he said.

"You mean Joe?"

"Aye, it's… well, I… it's just that you can do a lot better. Remember a girl's status depends on who she picks as a husband."

He turned to leave before the confusion furrowed my forehead. I wondered why Matthew disliked Joe all the way home, all night and for the next decade or so.

The family sat scattered around the living room intently watching the screen. This was before the novelty of the National Lottery wore off and most people dropped the unlikely daydream of becoming overnight millionaires. I looked at their individual faces, the intent expressions oblivious to the multi-coloured light flickering and caressing them. Mum and Dad held their tickets so tightly that I could see their thumbnails turning pale. Vanessa's nail polish brush was poised in mid-air. Even Marcus managed to be interested in something without boobs for more than ten minutes.

Evelyn's ARSE was still bugging me. It was present everywhere I went, entered my dreams and exited with each breath, only to return with the inhalation. I was absolutely positive I had definitely seen what I saw without a doubt.

Argh!

Suddenly everybody deflated. Marcus was the first to look over at me.

"Earth calling Genevieve, come in Genevieve."

"What's an arse when it's in a jar?" I asked absent-mindedly. My aim was not to cause a stir, I just needed to know and had been caught off-guard. There was silence for a moment while everybody stared at me.

"Oh my god, fucking weirdo," scowled Vanessa and stomped past me. The pieces of cotton wool between her toes popped out, irritating her even more.

"Language, Vanessa!" Dad bellowed.

"She swore first!" Vanessa screamed. "She said arse first!"

"Don't use that language in my house, Vanessa!" Mum screamed back, sounding very French.

I cowered by the sofa holding my breath. There was red flashing everywhere. I switched off to the noise, closed my eyes and felt myself being yanked upwards and across, dangling, warm turning to cold. I opened them again and found that I was in the front garden with Marcus.

"Did you bring me out here?"

"Yeah," he said throwing his head back to avoid setting his hair on fire as he lit a cigarette. He sucked on it and I saw every last bit of tension melt from his face as he inhaled deeply. The transformation was incredible to watch.

"What happened in there, Gene?" he asked gently. "I mean, you hardly ever open your gob and when you do, it's always cryptic."

The cigarette dangled from the corner of his mouth, somehow stuck fast to his bottom lip with invisible glue. Marcus always put his hands in his pockets whenever he held a conversation with anyone. He had the same casual slouch as Dad. This conversation was no different. Marcus had rounded his back and shoved his hands so deeply into his pockets that I could trace the bumpiness of his knuckles through the denim with my eyes.

"I don't know what happened. Vanessa hates me whatever I do or say and Mum thinks I'm mad. I'm not sure I fit in anywhere. Marcus, seriously, am I adopted?"

"No." He coughed.

"Then how come I'm different? I don't even look like any of you, don't understand what you all think or say, don't see the point of school or football..."

"Hold it, Gene," he said, holding up his hand as a sign to stop. "Sorry, Genevieve," he added when he saw the expression on my face. "You can't say things like 'arse in a jar' and expect people to take you seriously let alone understand what you're trying to say, right?"

I missed my cue to speak as I was far too busy watching the activity in the cloudiness surrounding Marcus. *Is this what confusion looks like?*

"Oy, Genevieve, what's arse in a jar?" he yelled.

I blinked to find Marcus' thumb and forefinger clicking in front of my face.

"A jar that says arse on it," I answered.

"One day I'll understand you," Marcus muttered under his breath. "And don't give a shit what Vanessa says, she just needs a good shag."

"What's a shag?"

"Bloody hell, never mind. Want to do something?"

"No thanks," I replied. I had begun to feel drained as I always did when Marcus was near me. *One day I may even understand you, big brother.*

I turned and walked in the direction of Canons Park where there were trees to talk to and comfort me. I suddenly felt guilty about my treatment of Marcus. He was alright but there was something about him that had a detrimental effect on my health and the only way I could protect myself was to push him as far away as I could.

Matthew introduced me to the fair when I was ten and almost every summer until I was sixteen he took me to see the spectacle. For six months of the year he would prepare the duke's horses to be shown. Preparation would begin after Christmas when horses would be chosen, groomed and trained. The sight of Matthew sitting on a stool and plaiting ribbons into their hair was a vision that brought a smile to my face for days. I burst into a prolonged fit of hysterical laughter the first time I witnessed it. Matthew poured a bucket of cold water over my head to calm me down but it didn't work. The laughter only died down when the aching in my stomach and face had become unbearable.

"What's amusing Genevieve?"

"You're plaiting hair!"

"Aye."

Silence. He watched as I rolled around on the ground.

"You're *plaiting*!"

"You're going to wake up to a sore belly."

I did but it only reminded me of the reason why I had laughed so hard in the first place and I chuckled to myself all morning and the next few mornings after.

Matthew offered to let me ride the ponies but I refused. They looked sweet and adorable and I was afraid that I might squash them. I was more than happy to take over their grooming, though, and loved seeing the silent answers to all my questions reflected in their soulful eyes. Matthew came to life during those summer fairs. It was a joy to see the pride on his face as he watched his horses trotting past, heads held regally high. He shaved and dressed up too, in a suit that was better than his Sunday suit, with cream breeches instead of his usual brown ones.

"Matthew, you've shaved!"

"Aye."

"And you've changed your clothes!"

"Aye."

"Why do you wear the same clothes for the rest of the year though?"

He looked blank.

"Did you have a bath before you wore your best?"

"Of course."

"Does that mean you don't bathe for the rest of the year?"

"Cheeky mare. Did your mother not teach you manners?"

"She tried. Didn't work though."

"Why not?"

"I'm stubborn!"

"Need a good hiding."

"Aye," I said, mimicking his voice.

Matthew deftly tied my ankles together with his belt and hung me upside down on the tree we were near. It took me the entire afternoon to free myself.

I discovered that the high vantage point that trees offered gave a wonderful new perspective of the traditional Edgware Fair. There were few buildings between the Chandos Estate and the High Street and I was able to observe the festivities quietly from where I perched. It was a noisy affair and the quiet streets of the sleepy old town heaved with excitement. In the distance I could make out the different settlements that must have been Burnt Oak, Mill Hill and possibly Totteridge. A huge house stood in the area I knew as Hale Lane, right at the top of the incline, and it was surrounded by lush farmland. Enormous bales of hay were being stacked on the land where my house later stood. I could see a row of men with pitchforks throwing them from carts onto the increasing mound. Long tables protected from the elements by makeshift tents were arranged towards the far side of the High Street towards Stonegrove and behind the church tower. Food was being served there from large cauldrons and the public houses that were dotted around had opened all their doors. I watched Matthew and four of his men lead the horses from the stables and walk them two-by-two through Canons Park and down Whitchurch Lane. Matthew saluted me before jogging up to the front of the line and leading the way. For the first time I noticed that his eyes were so pale that from that distance it looked like he had no irises at all.

Maybe Matthew is part zombie.

I looked at the scene in front and analysed every geographical detail.

Isn't it fascinating to see how it has all changed? The clues are all there. I mean, what was a tree-lined carriageway is now just a long, grassy mound in the park. The other entrance looks like it's now Du Cros Drive and the estate's been replaced by a school not even half its size. The churches are still there and so are the pubs. They haven't changed much.

"Matthew," I asked, when I noticed him hovering beneath me, "why are there so many churches here? You only really need one, right?"

"We're a simple farming community, Genevieve. We work hard and go to church every Sunday."

"And why are there so many public houses?"

"People need to get the news told to them, need to talk. Several folk come through here and need somewhere to stay and rest the horses on their way to London."

"Do you believe in God?"

"Aye. I'm a disciplined man."

"I'm supposed to be Catholic…"

Patient silence.

"…but I'm not sure about God. What it is, I mean."

"Everybody needs something to put their faith in. God will do nicely. Get down."

"Can't."

Matthew rolled his pale eyes and climbed up to get me. He looked even more like a zombie just then.

"Sometimes faith is all that will carry you through hard days. Genevieve, you will not be small forever - if you climb up, you learn to get down."

"Okay. You smell of hay."

"I work with horses."

"I want to be a farmer and work with horses too."

"No, you don't."

Buster's breathing was laborious and a funny wheezing sound seemed to pass out of his nostrils every time he exhaled. His glossy flank rose up and died down as if the blood beneath his skin had formed tidal waves. He reminded me of the old bellows that my grandmother had beside her fireplace, the ones that were too old to function properly. Poor Buster. For the past few years he'd been caught up in a vicious cycle from which his overdue death would be the only release. The arthritis had rendered him intermittently immobile, the lack of mobility was the root cause of his weight gain and the extra weight put added pressure on his painful joints. He was never in too much pain to wag his tail for me though. I loved him dearly for it.

Joe and I would take him for walks to Canons Park when he was comfortable enough to venture out. Once or twice Matthew had approached us and walked with us up to the back end of Canons Drive. Joe was oblivious to Matthew's presence but Buster knew he was there. His ears would perk up and his tail would get the vigorous workout that the rest of his body could not stand. Sometimes he would even try to put his paws on Matthew's spirit legs, only to come back down to earth with a little bump.

"Do you reckon he's getting randy?" Joe would ask, mystified by Buster's seemingly unprovoked excitement.

"No, I think he's just happy to be outside," I would answer whilst trying to stifle my laughter as Matthew slapped his forehead in mock exasperation.

I put my hand on Buster's ribcage and allowed it to gently rest there. A trickle of pink light passed from my arm to his torso. His leg twitched and his tail wagged, thumping softly on the kitchen tiles. I could sense his relief that he would not die alone. He began to whimper so I lay down beside him. The tile felt cool against my cheek and I could feel the soft caress of Buster's breath on my nose. A few minutes later it stopped. A small elliptical shard of light appeared briefly, standing out against the shadows of the net curtains, and rose up until I lost sight of it. Buster's soul had left his body. I didn't grieve his death, knowing that he was in a far better place now than he'd been in before.

At half past three, Joe burst in. When he saw me he stopped.

"Gen, he's on his way. The garage had a queue for tyres. Buster's already passed on hasn't he?"

"Yep."

Joe sat on the floor and held my hand.

Silence. The ticking clock sounded louder than usual. Joe looked at Buster's lifeless corpse, then at me, then at the corpse again. He didn't understand death and I could see his confusion. The smoky wisps slowly circled around his head clouding his thoughts. As he frowned I could just about make out a small conical form protruding from between his eyebrows but it seemed clogged and Joe was struggling to maintain clarity of thought. He looked at me and smiled. Suddenly the mist lifted.

"Do you think Buster's missing us?" he asked and squirmed a little.

"Oh no, he's in a much better place where things like that don't matter. There aren't any emotional burdens or obstacles, just lessons to be learned before he moves on. He's totally free and fluid. Got no unfinished business, see."

I stopped when I saw that Joe's confusion had returned.

"Just take it as a hunch, Joe."

Silence again.

"How long do you reckon before he's cold? Should we move him before he gets stiff?" Joe asked.

I did not answer him. I was far too fascinated by the grey-blue pulsations taking place around Joe's body. They occurred a few seconds apart in the same form as Joe but a bit away from him, as though he were encased in a larger Joe-shaped mesh. They made it look like he was wearing a special Spiderman outfit.

Our neighbour returned and immediately dropped to his knees beside Buster's body, picked him up and held him like a baby. He had lost his best friend of seventeen years and the heavy sadness that emanated from him gripped my entire torso.

"I think we'd better leave you to grieve in private. We're just next door and I'll keep the back door unlocked," I offered.

He nodded with sad eyes and spluttered an almost inaudible thank you. Joe and I left quietly without looking at one another. As we walked out of the back door I froze for a moment.

"Oh god! My grandmother's arrived and it's only Mum at home."

"How do you know?"

"I just do."

"So what? What's the big deal? There's someone to let her in."

"Joe, they hate each other. I've lost my grandmother once and I can't let it happen again."

Just before we both jumped over the fence I felt a small pang of an alien feeling.

"Don't ever die and leave me here, Joe."

"Promise."

When I was fourteen I had a dream and in that dream I saw a man who would be the protagonist in many a dream to come. He was quirky-looking and ever so slightly lanky. This is an extract from my dream diary:

I watch him as he sets up a tripod and camera in the middle of a large field. He ties his long hair in a ponytail and takes a deep breath, inhaling the essence of the beauty surrounding him. There is nothing else in the field except thousands and thousands of wheat sheaves that

ripple en masse before him. He smiles and takes several pictures of the
undulating yellow sea before moving the tripod to another location
and starting again. The man looks content and seems to blend in with
his surroundings. Every time I see him he gives me a feeling of déjà vu.

Mum had taken me to the doctor again, this time because of my lack of size.

"My other children were six inches taller at her age. My husband is over six feet and look how tall I am! Could Genevieve have dwarfism?"

"No, Mrs Kelly, she is perfectly in proportion and a normal height. Genevieve, do you eat properly?"

"I think so."

"But our families are bigger than this on both sides. There's no small relative she could have inherited from. She doesn't eat any meat, not even chicken. And she's so pale, doctor."

The doctor got up and walked over to me, torch ready. I noticed how he had developed little hammocks of skin under his eyes and that his fingers looked like uncooked chipolatas. *I wonder if he's made of pork...*

We were dismissed with a prescription for ferrous gluconate and instructions to visit the walk-in phlebotomy clinic at Edgware General Hospital.

"Anaemia," Mum announced at the dinner table, pointing at me.

"Anaemia, who?" asked Dad. "I thought her name was Genevieve. Isn't that right, Tiger?" Dad winked, I laughed and Vanessa rolled her eyes.

"I've made liver pate, creamed spinach and salad so you can have it with baguette. Shall I toast it for you?"

"I'm not hungry," Vanessa said and escaped quickly up the stairs.

"Vanessa!" Mum called after her. "It's not fattening, it's good for you, full of iron!"

"I'll eat the creamed spinach," I offered.

"Such a good girl," said Mum. "How much pate?"

"I don't eat pate."

"You have to."

"No."

"I say so, Genevieve."

"No."

"You have to grow."

"I won't eat it," I said, as firmly as I could without actually raising my voice, spreading my palms on the table on either side of my plate.

"Dad, is there any remote possibility that I was swapped at birth?"

"For god's sake, Tiger!" Dad's face went crimson with the effort of bellowing so loud. The skin around his eyes and lips remained white and he shook a little. It was very rare that Dad became this annoyed so I shut up and started to eat, out of respect, not fear.

"So stubborn, just like your father, Genevieve," added Mum. Her timing could not have been any worse if she'd practised it.

Dad threw Mum the filthiest look and we ate in silence. As Mum and Dad glared at one another from opposite ends of the dining table, I watched Margaret Davis stagger across the room clutching her stomach. The beads of perspiration that dotted her face gave away the pain she was racked with and her lips were tinged with blue. My heart went out to her but I was powerless to help. Eventually her pain subsided. She wiped her face, straightened her hair and managed to walk out upright.

Later, Mum and Dad were arguing again and I was sitting at the top of the stairs listening in the darkness. John Graham was crouched next to me listening too.

"She just stares into space!" Mum cried. "Sometimes I see her talking and laughing to herself. Don't you see it?"

"She's a child. They've always got things going on in those heads of theirs."

"No, she's different. There's something wrong with her! I'm her mother, I can sense it!" Mum was shrieking now.

"You sense nothing of the sort."

"It's your mother's influence! I told you I didn't want her back in our lives for good reason!"

"Don't you bring my mother into this!"

Upstairs I sat confused and intrigued, knowing that there was a definitive explanation for the questions I had about my grandmother's absence all those years. Even so, I couldn't listen to the whole argument. My search for answers was far outweighed by the emotional insult of what my mother thought of me.

"My parents argue too," John Graham sighed, "and my mother ends them by crying. They've started arguing a lot more often since…"

"…Evelyn flew into your lives on a broomstick!" I finished.

"Shhh! She'll hear you and I'll get a beating." John Graham looked around nervously and clasped his hands. Even in the darkness his blond hair shone a little. I had never been friends with an abused child before and the desperation in his eyes hurt me immensely.

It's easy to feel his fear but difficult to understand. I'm not really afraid of anything yet.

Below us, the fighting had reached a crescendo.

"Did you ever find out what happened to your brothers and sister?" I asked.

"No, I only stayed for you."

"Me? Wha..?"

Dad suddenly emerged from the living room and walked straight out of the front door. I heard the car start up and ran to the box room window to watch him pull out of the drive and zoom down the road. I may not have felt much in the way of fear but I certainly felt the first pangs of insecurity then.

Will you be back to call me Tiger? Please don't leave me alone with Mum and Vanessa.

I was far too interested in Matthew's background than was polite and he would remind me of this every time I initiated conversation. He answered all my questions without hesitation though and seemed to find great amusement in my obvious curiosity. He appeared to be so harsh and cold but there was something I liked about him. He had a good heart and there was nothing he could do to hide it. I saw less and less of my parents during the week. Recession hit, the price of everything increased and they were both working as many hours as they possibly could to afford things for us. As the months passed and our familiarity grew, Matthew became a surrogate parent.

My mother would often come up as a topic of discussion as she was becoming more and more vociferous regarding my odd behaviour. Although he was from a different time and rather set in his ways, he provided me with a sensible, objective opinion that only a caring adult could provide. It came straight from the heart and was invaluable to me.

"Matthew, did you ever have a mother?"

"Stupid question, Genevieve."

"But did you?"

"Aye, I had to be born of a mother like every child. I wasn't born old."

"Really? Just kidding. But did you know her?"

"No."

"Why?"

"Why does it make you so curious?"

"I want to know, that's all. Please."

"She passed on when I was not yet walking. Didn't survive the cold, I was told."

"Do you miss her?"

"No."

Matthew was sitting opposite me on a large chunk of tree trunk. There were several of them scattered around this part of the field where we sat. I traced my finger along the deep groove that the axe had made in the block next to me. Matthew kept the axes locked up behind the stables. He simply could not risk his horses being stolen or the duke's estate being robbed.

"Who brought you up then, Matthew?"

"My father."

"Do you ever miss him?" He looked at me and hesitated.

"Aye."

"What kind of things did you do together?"

"Stop asking questions."

"Can't."

"You can."

"No, really, I can't. It'll go round and round in my head until I lose sleep."

"Lunacy, Genevieve. You're a lunatic."

"I know. But what was there to do in your time?"

"I learned to ride horses and was taught the trade when I was older."

"Did you go to school?"

"Aye. Not like you, mind."

"What do you mean?" Matthew sighed without moving. I was not going to leave him alone today and he knew it.

"I was an apprentice, Genevieve."

"Can you read and write?"

"Aye."

"Count?"

"Aye. Can you stop asking questions?"

"I'll try. What did you do when you had a day off and your father had a day off? What did you do together?"

Bicycles, rollerskates and ice cream had not been invented in Matthew's day and I was very curious to know how he had filled his time. It was hard enough imagining Matthew as a child, let alone having fun.

"He took me to Tyburn on occasion."

"Where's that?"

"London. We watched the hangings there."

For the first time in a long time, I was totally lost for words.

"Become quiet I see. Not something you're used to?"

I gulped back the sickness that had begun to pool in my throat.

"What… what was it like?" I ventured.

Matthew looked at me for a moment. I could tell he was thinking but that was as much as his deadpan face would concede. At length he answered. It was planned to soften the shock of what I had just heard.

"It was only a little worse than buying pigs."

Five months previously Matthew had taken me to the pig market at Finchley. He'd seemed reluctant at first but I'd had such a wonderful time at Barnet Fair the summer before that I begged him constantly, month after month, to take me with him to the pig market. One day he became so fed up that he agreed, in a fit of rage. I had held him to it.

"The pig market is no place for a decent young lady. Stray more than a hair's breadth from me and I'll tan your backside when we get home."

"Okay," I chirped.

The pig market was not an open-air affair of happy, teeming civilisation. It was mainly held indoors within the confines of sheds and outhouses. It was dark, claustrophobic and had the racy atmosphere of illegal cock fighting. By now I was used to the smell of horse manure and burning hay. My well-seasoned nose no longer relayed the shock of smelling poo - which had once caused me to retch uncontrollably - back to my brain in the same way. However, the dingy, stagnant atmosphere of those poky sheds had fermented the stench of pig to produce a concentrated air of putrefaction that punched the oxygen out of my lungs and brought tears to my eyes. When I could not hold my breath any longer, I slipped outside, hoping to have inhaled a lungful of fresh air and returned before Matthew had noticed I was missing.

It was a chilly but clear day outside and there were several people milling around in the open. Some were leading pigs along the muddy pathways between buildings, others were drunk and looking for non-existent people outside the two small alehouses nearby.

"Pretty child, I have something for you."

The man next to me was immense. He was wider than he was tall and the effort of carrying his belly around with him had caused droplets of sweat to run down his face, even in the cold. He was very ugly with bulbous features and rotten teeth. His clothes smelled of alcohol and stale body odour.

"Come with me, I'll show you something fit for a lady."

"No, I don't want to see it, thanks."

"Why, you impertinent little…"

"You wasted your energy, not me. If you'd asked whether I wanted to see it in the first place, I wouldn't have had to be rude."

"A mannerless child is the devil's child."

"A stupid man is a waste of space."

"I said come with me, child."

He grabbed my arms and tried to drag me towards him but I wriggled free. He was too drunk and slow to catch hold of me again. It was not until this moment that I noticed the thinner man with him. He lunged forward and I ducked, causing him to fall into the muck. I picked up two handfuls of crap from the ground, threw them into their eyes and slipped back into the pig shack through a gap in the door. I must have resumed my position just as Matthew noticed I was missing.

"Genevieve," he growled, "where...?"

"I fell over. I was behind you the whole time but I fell, see."

"Aye, I believe you." He sounded utterly unconvinced and put his hands on his hips, expecting more lies. I showed him my dirty palms as proof. "I lost a bid on that sow because of you." He nodded to a filthy, snorting bag of fat with no discernible features other than a snout. I had never seen such a huge pig.

"Just as well. She's one porker of a fat pig!"

"Exactly."

Once we were outside, Matthew found an abandoned pitcher of ale, now diluted with rainwater, and made me wash my hands in it.

"Shake them quickly before they get cold," he ordered.

That had been my adventure at Finchley's pig farm and I learned to trust Matthew's judgement after that. He really did have my best interests at heart.

Now as he sat watching me, I began to wonder whether I interested him by challenging his views on how young ladies should be or whether I had misjudged him from the very beginning. Sometimes he came across as chauvinistic but often the divide that should have existed between us would simply disappear once we started talking. Each gave the other their due respect and I appreciated the basic sense of identity that gave me.

Matthew didn't take his eyes off me as he unwrapped the parcel of food and laid it out on the wooden stump directly in front of us both. He spread out the small rolls, herb butter, cold meat and cheese and the handkerchief of blackberries and invited me to tuck in. I always waited for him to pick something.

"Ladies first," Matthew said, as he threw me a roll and handed me his personal knife.

We ate facing one another, staring directly at the other's face as we chewed. Although the arrangement appeared confrontational, nothing could be further from the truth. It was familiar and comfortable, unique to Matthew. His eyes were hard as steel but not searching or judgmental, only quietly observant. He did not speak whilst eating, just like I hated noise, so our mealtimes were silent, almost spiritual. This time, however, he surprised me by saying something.

"You will not understand them until you have your own."

"Who?"

"Your mother and father."

"What makes you say that?"

"Because you have not yet happily sacrificed anything for someone."

"Did you like being a father?"

"Was for too short a time. Can't say."

"And then I came along to disturb the peace!"

"Aye."

I flashed Matthew my biggest grin. Matthew's eyes smiled back at me warmly, but the rest of his face did not even twitch.

SEVEN

Reality Strikes

*If I weren't a freak in the first place,
I certainly feel like one now.*

Our GP's office stank of Dettol and coffee. There was a locum in today and Mum was not happy. The poor girl must have graduated that year and gave me the most nervous and feeble examination. She then fiddled with my notes a little, shuffling and reshuffling the papers around, until Mum lost her patience and launched a barrage of questions at her. I had lost interest in my mother and did not even look at her when she tried to speak to me, let alone listen. She had interpreted the loss of me in her own way; there was something seriously wrong with me and it could be fixed medically. After that I would go back to being her daughter again. But what exactly did that mean? Was I not hers whatever my condition?

I watched all of Mum's interactions very closely when she was least aware. They were always tinged with anger and frustration and I felt somehow that, although the anger was directed at somebody else, it originated within and had nothing to do with any outside party. She had begun to slouch a little and it wasn't due to her age. Her bubble was dark and full of small eddying currents that were localised in certain areas of her body. On her upper back was a blob that weighed her down. When she ranted, bits would break off and travel upwards, giving her a headache. It looked as though the weight of the world was on her shoulders. I noticed how different the arguments between Mum and Dad and between Mum and Vanessa were. When Mum fought with Vanessa there were fireworks and it was frightening being in the same room as them, as one could get caught up in the crossfire quite literally. Absorbing those poisoned darts was painful and made me want to cry. However, when Mum fought with Dad, the connection between their hearts remained visible and intact, and no nasty daggers were hurled at the other. Mum's blob became smaller during her fights with Dad, but with Vanessa it became bigger. I fed it too, even without managing to argue, and I felt guilty about it.

The doctor offered to write me a referral to a sleep therapist after noticing my dark circles. Mum was not impressed and promptly stood up, grabbed me and left.

"Thank you!" I called, as I was shoved through the door.

Outside the surgery, Mum told me to walk home as she had to buy groceries. I walked to Joe's house instead.

Joe and I sat on his desk, throwing paper balls at his neighbour who was gardening below. We would intermittently duck behind the curtains as he looked up at the window and quietly cursed his invisible enemy.

"I might go and see a sleep therapist," I said.

"What and why?" Joe was adding Maltesers to some of the paper missiles.

"Not really sure but I have dark circles."

"I never noticed them and I know your face well," Joe said. He blushed when he realised what he'd just said and threw a handful of paper-covered Maltesers out of the window.

"Don't waste decent chocolate, Joe," I chided, salvaging what was left in the box.

Ravi burst in and hurled some paper balls at us. *Attacked with our own ammunition, the shame of it.*

"I've got my sodding A Levels soon. Don't disturb the neighbours, so they don't disturb me!" he roared.

Neither Joe nor I said anything as Ravi stood in front of us breathing heavily. Our lack of reaction pushed him over the threshold of anger and he lunged at Joe. I fell off the desk as they rolled by, a ball of fists and legs, looking like the personification of stupidity. I caught sight of a bottle of water behind the curtain and poured it over them, hoping to shock them into leaving each other alone. It did.

"What's that smell?" asked Ravi.

"Nothing. Get out of my room," ordered Joe, fixing his gaze a lot lower than he should have. His reaction was a little out of the ordinary and took me by surprise.

I looked at the bottle in my hand. Vodka.

Ravi had taken off his vodka-soaked clothes and marched out. I looked at Joe.

"Joe?"

"I just wanted to try it. It's no big deal is it?"

Joe proceeded to strip in my presence and all was forgotten. *You look so much better without clothes on.* I gulped and left the room.

Contrary to reason, I slept very fitfully at the sleep clinic, so fitfully that I was suspected of wasting their time and was prematurely discharged. Nobody said anything but I could read the hidden messages in their smiles and sense the whisperings in their heads. Mum was livid. Her latest theory had been: *Genevieve has been driven mad by lack of sleep and she cannot sleep because there is something wrong with her.* As usual I had embarrassed her and she felt that I'd done it on purpose.

"I know what you kids think of me," she spat on the way home. "Stupid foreign mother with stupid Catholic beliefs. Even Vanessa treated me like an imbecile. I wish I'd never had children! I could have had a proper career in fashion or managing a company instead of you ingrates."

I wish I knew what had made her so bitter. My mother's bitterness was something that had grown with time and experience. It seemed to have thrived like a fungus. It was her personal disease that had begun many years ago, even before I was born. *What exactly makes a person bitter? And is this what we all have to look forward to in life?*

"See! You just sit in silence. Never talk to me do you? Sometimes I wonder if you are alive in reality." She was thinking in French and directly translating into English, an indication of an angry rant that would last the whole journey home. I closed my eyes and wondered what Joe was doing.

The pattern on the glass looked pretty as the red liquid swirled around inside, producing a marbling effect before settling. Towards the end it bubbled a little. It was the same colour as my mother's university ball gown, the one she'd worn when she met my father for the first time. It was a similar colour to Vanessa's hair. Joe's favourite colour was red. But red was the one colour I refused to wear, as I was unsettled by it.

"Hellooo?" A hand was waving in front of my face.

"Eh?"

"You're all done and can go now."

The phlebotomist put my blood on the top row of neatly stacked trays and taped cotton wool to my arm. The name labels were not stuck down properly and the ends were jutting off the sides of the test tube. I longed to press them down.

"Genevieve, you can go now."

Joe was waiting outside for me with his eyes clamped shut. He had done the same thing when we got our BCG injections years ago, before falling to the floor. He had a phobia of needles and didn't want to humiliate himself again this time by fainting.

"Do you want to go back to school or down to the shops?" he asked as he flashed his cheekiest grin. I was amazed at how white his teeth looked against his tanned skin.

"Back to school, Joe. We have English today."

"Exactly." Joe grimaced. We were silent for a while until Joe asked, "Why are you having yet another blood test?"

"Because I'm puny and strange and Mum thinks there's something wrong with me, like I've got the wrong genes or something."

We were standing beside a mirrored window and I caught a glimpse of my reflection. A small bubble of frustration was rising up from my chest. I knew that the moment it touched my throat I would begin to cry. I could feel the lump and I swallowed several times to push it down again until I was out of the uncontrollable crying danger zone. My stomach began to knot instead.

"Well, there's the height issue," Joe was prattling on without looking at me, thank goodness, "but you're just petite and you look a bit like your great uncle, whatever he was called. I mean, he's not as deathly pale as you…"

"Oh shut it!" I took Joe's arm as we walked on.

He stopped suddenly.

"I was only kidding Joe. I didn't mean to tell you to shut up."

"No, no. Isn't that your friend?"

I looked in the direction of his pointed finger. On the opposite side of the road, a girl was pushing a pram carrying a screaming new-born infant. She had a swollen abdomen, greasy hair and a tired expression. She looked very familiar but it took me a few seconds to remember her name. *Mongo.*

"How the mighty have fallen," Joe grinned.

"Joe, come on."

"It makes me wonder who'd want to put a bun in her oven in the first place." He looked absolutely disgusted.

"Do you think she consciously chose that or went along with the flow of destiny?" I was thinking back to the kidney bean I saw with her. It must have been the embryo that had not yet been conceived.

"Who'd choose that?" Joe was incredulous.

"If that were me, Mum would have killed me."

"If it happens to us, I'll marry you," Joe mocked.

"My previous statement still stands – shut it!"

"My previous statement still stands," Joe squawked, mocking me again.

"Seriously Joe, do you think people really have choices or have to go through a certain destiny?"

"Dunno. Maybe we have to go through things and our choices are already made. It would be a lot easier for God. Otherwise he'd be inventing scenarios for so many little choices. There'd be millions of destinies per person."

Joe did not believe in God and it had begun to sound a little bit like sarcasm. I wasn't convinced by his theory, it sounded like a cop-out to assume that we have no real choices in life, but I didn't want to turn this into an argument. I could sense that Joe was becoming tetchy. The pins he had created around him were beginning to poke me uncomfortably.

"Okay," I said and took his arm again as we walked on.

Michael Davis passed away before his wife. He'd been in terrible agony when he died, vomiting blood and running a fever so high that Margaret was worried that his insides had burned to cinders. It must have been a blessed relief to himself and all around him when his soul finally left his wasted body. Immediately, Evelyn had accused Margaret and her children of bringing back strange diseases from the tropics. She did not even show the faintest hint of mercy as Margaret wasted away and eventually succumbed to the same symptoms as her husband.

"I wish I'd been alive to comfort my mother," John Graham said. The sorrow and bitterness were evident in his voice even after all these years. He stared into the distance. "She died alone. Even my sister and brothers weren't allowed to say goodbye. Evelyn had sent them away already. She never saw them again."

"How did the old bat explain it?"

"She told everybody that my mother couldn't cope after the loss of my father and one of her children and that she'd begun to deteriorate mentally too. My mother was only ever driven mad by her terrible stomach pains and she made sure her children didn't see her cry."

"How do you know this?" I enquired gently.

"I've always been with her. She was my mother, Genevieve."

John Graham began to cry. He sobbed softly at first, poking little fingers behind his spectacles to wipe the tears away, but before long streams of tears were gushing down his cheeks in tiny rivulets, turning them red. To my horror, he began to howl loudly. I understood then that he had never had the opportunity to mourn for his mother or come to terms with her death.

That night I lay in bed, wide awake, anticipating a nightmare. Before long that strange feeling of zooming began to take over, tugging and pulling me out of my physical body and up through the roof, into the night sky. As if flung out of a catapult, I travelled across the sky so fast that my non-existent stomach flipped over several times before I came to a halt, hovering in the well-lit living room of a large and spacious house, somewhere in the midst of the rolling English countryside.

A young man with a ponytail was arguing with someone, a slim old man with a good head of hair and a really sad brown jacket. He had the same physique as the young man but their faces did not look alike at all. The furniture in the room was old-fashioned and very twee, like the home of a high court judge or a distinguished doctor is expected to be. The young man was standing behind a chair, tracing circles in the wood with his index finger. I watched as his long, tapered digit moved around, the almond-shaped nail turning white at the end where he was applying pressure. I smiled at him but he didn't see me.

"You stupid boy! Photography? What use is bloody photography?"

The young man's face was burning red and his lanky frame straightened in defence.

"I never wanted to be a doctor."

He spoke softly and I smiled again in appreciation. *He hates noise, just like me. Either that or he's too vexed to give a shit about raising his voice.*

"I'm not paying your fees anymore. You can pay me back for the last four years from your photographer's wages, if you can!"

"I haven't touched it, so you can have it." *Principles too! Well done, Mr Ponytail.*

"Don't tell me you've been spending your mother's inheritance! She'd turn in her grave."

"She'd be proud of me." *I think so too, Mr Ponytail.*

"Get out of my sight and don't you dare come crawling back!"

Mr Ponytail took a deep breath and calmly walked out. As he passed me I tried to reach out and touch him but couldn't – I didn't seem to have any arms. He hesitated for a moment and for that split second he looked straight at me without seeing me. He had a rare sensitivity in his eyes, the type only artists have, and I was certain I knew him from somewhere. To my dismay I was sucked away from him, only to wake up in my bed feeling tired and breathless.

I hardly ever slept in on Saturdays, even on the numerous occasions that I hadn't slept at all. Saturday morning had become martial arts morning, and I would begin to look forward to the next class the moment the preceding one had ended. Originally, my intention had been to learn how to defend myself against the bullies at school and channel any anger that might arise as a result. However, as the months passed, it became a form of personal meditation for me, long before I even knew what meditation was. I became aware of the mechanics of my body, my confidence grew and my appetite increased, much to the delight of my mother.

I remember too clearly for comfort the day the class was cancelled. It was the day that my mother became convinced I suffered from some kind of paranoia and there followed an epic battle to try and change her stubborn perception. I lost that battle, or gave it up somewhere along the way. This particular Saturday I jumped out of bed as per my usual routine, ate, showered, dressed and ran down the roads parallel to Honeypot Lane towards my 9 o'clock class.

NO CLASS TODAY. SORRY FOR SHORT NOTICE.

WIFE HAD BABY ALL DOING WELL.

NEXT SATURDAY AS NORMAL.

I sighed with the anti-climax and walked home again, dragging my feet. Joe would be at football practice, Vanessa was gone and Mum and Dad had left early to beat the crowds at Brent Park Tesco. Marcus would be dead to the world until 3pm but at least he was at home. Recently, the thought of Marcus made me grin with amusement. Gone were the long hair, unkempt style and stubbled jaw. Marcus was a yuppie now and wore a crisp suit to his city job. He slept in at weekends as his new work routine was tiring him out. Dad was convinced he had a form of jet lag due to the very late nights he enjoyed during university.

Marcus is a banker now. Joe and I reckon that's just a flash way of saying wanker. Apparently, it's all about power lunches, making money and being a prat.

Luckily, Marcus had a sense of humour (the only positive character trait that Mum would attribute to Dad's side of the family) and played along with the wanker jokes, standing straight and sticking one finger up at us in jest when Mum wasn't looking.

As I turned onto Whitchurch Lane, I began to feel light-headed. The static began to crackle in my inner ears and I stopped at the front door momentarily to blink myself back to earth. To my horror, the entire house had vanished and I was left standing in a patch of mud next to a large shack. There was a loud pounding coming from inside along with an intense heat escaping from under the thick curtain that covered the entrance. I walked around the shack, aware that standing still was making me sink deeper into the mud. There was a small cluster of similar buildings nearby and livestock were running around freely.

"Forget where am I, *when* am I?" I said aloud, perhaps hoping for an answer to come out of the sky and make everything seem less nonsensical. I stood still until my impatience gave me some courage. "Sod this. I'm exploring."

I pushed aside the entrance covering and peered into the darkness inside. There were tools lined up against the wall beside me and other implements I didn't recognise, some of which were glowing with the intense heat of the molten metal being poured into a mould. It looked like an orange ghost and I watched for a second.

"A blacksmith?" I asked aloud.

I had surprised the man inside. His surprise turned to anger and he strode through the piles of objects, banging his tools down on the table and throwing off his gloves. As he came closer, he let forth expletives in an alien language. I understood everything he said because of the vibrational energy of his words.

"You stupid child! It's dangerous in here! Get out!"

That was all I could make out before he smacked me really hard across my face. My cheek and lip tingled and I could feel them swelling straight away. Tears welled up in my eyes and my dignity

told me to escape before he saw them. I turned to flee and tripped over something flat and soft - the living room rug. I was home.

"You alright, Tiger?" Dad and Mum were back.

"Genevieve, help us to put these things in the kitchen," said Mum gently. "I want to start cooking for Marcus before he wakes up. Otherwise he eats cornflakes for lunch." She picked up a Tesco bag and disappeared past the doorframe. She hadn't noticed my injured face. I followed them into the kitchen.

"Haven't either of you noticed my face?"

"Can't not with a mug as pretty as yours, Tiger."

"Thanks Dad. No, I mean it's swollen."

"Genevieve," sighed Mum. "There is nothing wrong with your face."

I ran up the stairs just as Mum uttered the word 'paranoia'. *That's strange. He hit me so hard and I felt it. I honestly felt it swell.*

I stood in front of the full-length mirror in Vanessa's room and concentrated.

Why did I not think of this earlier? I can see everybody else's.

Last year I had noticed a small black blob in my bubble, a little to the left of my diaphragm. At first I had mistaken it for a stain on my t-shirt. I had worn plain white this time just to be sure. The small black blob had become a cone or hole, almost as though something had burrowed into my bubble. It was about eighteen inches from my abdomen.

I knew exactly what it was.

I will bide my time.

Philip had attacked me with a cricket bat in the changing rooms after hearing the results of the cricket team try-outs. The school was fielding a mixed team that year and I had beaten a dozen other wicket-keeping hopefuls. Several members of my class had noticed me for the first time and offered their congratulations, making me wonder why I hadn't taken an interest in cricket earlier. Normally I would opt for the loner's sport like long distance running or gymnastics, but Joe had pressed me to try cricket as he wanted to share his love of sport with me in some capacity. I had been aware of Philip's jealousy for an hour or so before the team was announced. He appeared with a muddy green tint to him which confused me at first because I thought he looked nauseous. Every few minutes he would turn towards me and whisper threats, making a fist to bring to my attention the violence he would inflict on me later.

"Hey freak! I'm going to beat the weirdness out of you." I ignored him. "You'd better not be on the team `cos I'm goin' to make cricket practice your worst nightmare." I knew he wouldn't make the team but I didn't know that I would. "Better not get in my way, freak."

Philip's arrogance was so great that he didn't even wait for the changing room to clear before he swung the bat at me and bruised my ribcage badly. Joe lunged forward trying to protect me but the damage had already been done. I did not allow myself to cry, but as I was led away I prayed with all my heart that Philip would never have children. *Please God, don't let the bastard reproduce. Don't let him inflict his evil spawn on society. Just in case other kids in the future are subjected to this. My ribs really hurt.*

If I could have been granted any wish at that moment, it would have been exactly that. I thought long and hard for reasons as to why Philip should hate me so much that he would want to damage me. Violence was something I did not comprehend.

The next day Mum decided that it was a good idea to buy me my first bra. I did not have anything to fill it up with yet, but I thought it might give us the opportunity to do something that normal people do. Vanessa came too as she had, once again, rapidly outgrown her own underwear. The prospect of my first bra excited me unexpectedly. I had never even tried one on before and had only seen them on washing lines, advertisements or in the laundry. They were the gatekeepers of womanhood and I was at the threshold. Just before we got into the car, Mum made us take our coats off and stand straight in front of her.

"Hmm, 34C," she said, looking at Vanessa. "32A, if that," she said to me.

Vanessa smirked. If I'd known what that meant I would have died of embarrassment.

The bra-fitter at Marks and Spencer was a matronly lady who was a little too matronly to fit inside the cubicle with me. She handed me a selection of 'training' bras and stepped outside, whisking the curtains back across the cubicle entrance to protect my modesty. I held one of the bras in my hands, turning it over to examine it carefully. I wasn't sure what I expected from it – the term 'training' bra immediately brought to mind stabilisers or scaffolding but this bra looked perfectly normal to me. I took off my shirt and put the bra on before realising that there was no mirror in the cubicle. They were outside.

Do I step out in my smalls? Nah, Vanessa will only take the piss out of my non-boobs anyway. Best stay put. What a daft idea, having the mirrors outside. What does the A mean anyway? How does one measure a boob? By hand? Everyone's got different-sized hands though. Suddenly, the curtain swished aside to reveal my mother.

"What is taking so... oh, oh, oh... what happened to you, Genevieve?" she screamed.

"Eh?"

My mother had started to cry and was hyperventilating.

"What the hell's going on?" cried Vanessa, rushing towards us in her underwear, a tape measure dangling from her armpit.

"Jesus!" she said as she looked at my torso.

"I'm not that small!" I cried, beginning to feel humiliated.

"No, wally, look!"

Vanessa pointed to my ribcage. The purple stripes looked strangely beautiful against my pale skin. The darker ones directly over my ribs were interspersed with paler ones in between. I hadn't thought it necessary to tell my parents about Philip hitting me with the bat and didn't expect the bruising to be so bad. Showering that morning had hurt but I hadn't had time to examine the wound, especially seeing as it was tucked away beneath my arm and down my side. It was horrendous and I could understand why my mother was panicking.

"Mum, it's fine. I'm not in much pain, see." I flapped my arms for a few seconds, hoping she would stop crying but to no avail.

"Is everything alright?" asked the female security guard who had just walked into the fitting rooms.

"No," said my mother, clearly shaken and wiping her eyes.

"You're causing quite a commotion. Has anyone stolen your purse?"

"No, I don't care about a stupid purse! Somebody has been hitting my daughter and I don't know who it was. She won't tell me!"

"It's just a school bully, Mum. I'll be alright."

"We're going to the police this time, Genevieve, whether you like it or not."

Later that afternoon, I was examined by a police doctor and had x-rays and photographs taken of my bruised ribs. The school authorities moved swiftly, interviewing pupils who had witnessed the violence and then expelling Philip from school permanently. It did not help matters though. Philip would often be waiting outside the gates for his sister, hissing threats at me under his breath as I walked past. Once or twice he tried to trip me up or throw something at me. Eventually, when Joe grew bigger and Ravi or Marcus were around to walk me home, Philip slunk back into the shadows where he could no longer physically touch me. But he could still haunt me in my nightmares.

The chopped fruit in front of me was going brown. I was looking at it but it didn't register. I was wide awake this time and could clearly see Mr Ponytail in front of me. He was sobbing. I had never seen a grown man cry before and found the sight rather intriguing. It was different to female crying. He was silent but his eyes were wet and he made no attempt to wipe his snotty nose. The table in front of him was covered with photographs. He picked one up, looked at it and held it against his heart. A big gulp emerged from his throat. Soon he was wailing inconsolably. I felt the shockwaves of his sorrow and I began to cry too.

"Tiger, what's wrong?" Dad was horrified. He'd never seen me cry before. My pride had always prevented me from crying in front of witnesses, even when spanked. Crying had always been a private affair, until now.

Drat. How do I explain this one?

"Nothing, Dad. I'm just a bit fed up."

"With what? Mum?"

"I'm fed up of going to the doctor, counsellor, sleep specialist, psychiatrist, everybody. If I weren't a freak in the first place, I certainly feel like one now."

"Okay, I'll make sure Mum leaves you alone. Have you told her all this?"

"No."

"Well, she may be almost superhuman but she's not quite psychic. Trust me, thirty years on and she still doesn't know when to leave me in peace to watch the footy."

That night my parents had another blazing row. Dad spent the next few nights on the sofa and I spent the next few years feeling guilty.

The blacksmith was a strange-looking man who wore a tunic made from a rough material the colour of onion skin. It was slightly softer than sackcloth and quite worn, with tiny tufts sticking out of it around the edges and where it covered joints. He wore boots that resembled tatty casts and his knees were bare. My gaze followed the weaving path of criss-crossed laces that held the boot securely to his leg. There was no excess skin that protruded in between the mesh pattern but some ragged bits were overflowing from the top.

He put his tools down and walked over to a pot on the open fire. As he lifted the pot, the flames jumped up and illuminated his face. There were deep furrows in his forehead and his eyes had retreated back into their sockets. I could sense his exhaustion and the odd sensation of stale fear, long since accepted and buried deep within his psyche. His body language was the epitome of dejection and weariness with stooping shoulders, drooping eyes and curved spine. He couldn't have been that old, maybe thirty-odd, but his eyes told me that his real life had ended years before he died.

"I'm so tired," he told me in that unrecognisable language I somehow understood.

"Talk to me about it all," I replied.

He handed me a thick cup full of hot liquid. I could not tell what the cup was made from in the darkness but I think it was wood. The concoction smelled foul, like moss, and I braced myself as I took a tiny sip. It was some kind of herb tea and tasted fine. *Phew! I can't be rude when he's so upset.*

"All we do is work all day. The hours are long and the taxes high. We can barely afford to live. They make us work to the death."

"Who?"

"The Romans. So far I've made two hundred spear heads but haven't been paid for more than fifty. My beloved wife died of exhaustion years ago and I buried her outside with my dagger and brooch. I pray she's rich and looked after where she is."

"How old are you?"

"Twenty-five. I feel like an old man."

Suddenly I felt sorry for him. As a general rule I don't feel pity for others, having a huge sense of pride myself. I hate embarrassing people and pity can reduce somebody to the size of a pinhead. But something deep within his eyes seared a little wound in my heart. The utter hopelessness and loss of identity was so painfully evident in every molecule of his existence.

I would remember him in the years to come when I would fight for whatever cause it was I believed in at the time.

EIGHT

Beneath The Surface

I watched the expletives leave my mouth in physical form…
One of them hit the woman really hard
between the breasts…

Whenever any local church had a fete or cake sale, Mum made sure that Vanessa and I were there. I could understand her hope that religion might be a positive and grounding force in a way-ward teenager's life, but I didn't understand how a cake sale could achieve that. Also, none of our local churches was Catholic, which ordinarily should have given my mother cause for suspicion. She must have been desperate because at this point any church seemed just as good as a Catholic one.

"Religion is very important, girls," she would announce, just before we got to the gate. And then, looking at Vanessa, "It gives you a sense of self-respect and humility."

I did not escape her subtle disapproval either. "Genevieve, it will give you mental peace and something to focus on."

"I have books and Joe for that, Mum."

Vanessa would smirk and Mum would grab us and drag us through the gate, cursing in French and reminding us not to speak in English if we were going to say something stupid. Heaven forbid that anybody should blame her for any misdirected sarcasm from myself or bad humour from Vanessa. These church gatherings were the rare times that Vanessa and I crudely and temporarily bonded. Sometimes during the summer, Marcus would join us. Mum would bribe him with promises of roast dinners and apple crumble if he carried all her purchases home. She would then extend the bribe to manageable, individual portions that he could freeze and thaw later if he kept an eye on us the whole time. It was a lot more enjoyable having Marcus as company. He held great entertainment value although Vanessa and I were often blamed for the consequences of his antics.

These outings to church fairs became more unbearable after the age of thirteen. I had started my period that winter and the combination of fluctuating hormones, school and my personal cravings for solitude meant that crowds and small talk with strangers was very difficult. During my weekends, I wanted to be alone or free to follow my own pursuits. My mother took this as a sign that I was going off-track and becoming withdrawn. She actively encouraged me to keep busy by accompanying her everywhere to do everything that came naturally to a forty-seven year old. I didn't understand her tactics at all - I was a sensible child and never went out of my way to give her grief as Vanessa did, so why didn't she leave me alone?

"Why do you nag me all the time, Mum? You never nag Vanessa," I would argue, when I could be bothered to.

"Are you on drugs, Genevieve? I work at the NHS, I know the signs of a drug dependency, remember that."

Where was the point in arguing with that? It was easier to tag along and pretend to be listening to her.

Hormones opened up a Pandora's Box of feelings that I had

been oblivious to for the first thirteen years of my life. I slept a lot more. I would go to bed irritated and wake up irritated. Television programmes could upset me. I discovered my libido - Joe was in my thoughts almost constantly and I began to notice things about him that indulged my heightened senses. His skin was smooth to touch. He had muscles on his legs that were attractive to stare at. His throaty laugh and his broken voice made my skin erupt in goose pimples. Even more strange and startling was how different I became to my sister. Puberty had turned Vanessa into a preening swan that talked all the time in whining and manipulative tones, whereas I ended up at the other end of the spectrum, shunning every beauty aid except my comb and refusing to use my voice box unless I had to. In fact I had no interest in anything that an average teenage girl would describe as a rite of passage, such as alcohol and cigarettes. My outlets were art, books, hiking and the company of my friends. For the most part I was happy, although the scales would tilt at the smallest provocation and I would struggle to find the balance again.

Unfortunately, puberty affected me in a way that most other teenagers would never experience. It wrought havoc with the way I saw the world and I became sensitised to other people at a level where I could not protect myself. Crowds terrified me.

That's why I came to depend on Marcus to save me from Mum during the church fairs. Marcus had the privilege of being able to exert his will and get away with it. He often told my mother that we were leaving early and dragged us away with him without waiting for her comment or reaction. He not only saved me from boredom but also my mother from humiliating public arguments with Vanessa in the presence of God.

On one occasion, Marcus grabbed a book that Vanessa was about to hurl at my mother across a graveyard full of stalls and silver-haired bargain veterans. He pulled her out of the graveyard by her hair before she'd had a chance to scream abuse at him and beckoned for me to follow the moment Mum had taken her eyes off us. It was a great day for a walk, or so I thought. Marcus had just been paid and offered to buy us beer on the way home. Vanessa refused on the grounds that her figure would suffer and I was just not interested in a drink that looked like it had been pissed out that morning. Instead we decided to walk up Stonegrove and take the back route through Canons Drive. That way Marcus could throw a couple of pebbles in the pond and wee in the bushes.

I first noticed the fat, angry woman near the nursery on Stonegrove. She was out of breath, flushed and sweaty and had her eyes fixed on the potted shrubbery that graced the entrance. Beside her stood a skinny, mousy-haired teenager wearing nothing but faded jeans and a bikini top that barely covered her mosquito-bite breasts. I had a feeling of foreboding as we moved closer to them and there was something about the woman that gave me a feeling of deja vu. Marcus and Vanessa didn't seem to notice the change in the atmosphere as we walked past them, far too busy arguing over Marcus' last cigarette.

"What were you staring at?" screeched the woman as soon as we'd passed by.

"Don't say anything," said Marcus, taking our arms and guiding us towards the curb to cross the road. But the woman had grabbed my other arm and pulled me back.

"What, do you think we're like your servants or something?" asked the girl, moving her head from side to side like a pigeon. She moved closer to my face and I could see the details of her pasty skin, the tiny spots covering her chin and jaw. Her mascara was crumbling off her lashes and peppering her cheeks.

"Pardon?" I said, stepping back.

I had no idea what they wanted from me. I became aware of a football-sized bubble, the colour of dried blood, which had emanated from the woman and floated towards Marcus. It hovered near his abdomen until his stomach sucked it up and it disappeared from my view. I watched his expression change from simple annoyance to demonic rage. His face darkened and he stood up tall, stepping a little closer to the woman so that he was looking down on her.

"Get your filthy hands off my sister!" he roared. "Don't touch her!"

Vanessa, standing next to Marcus, flared up too.

"Who the hell would want to stare at your ugly face, you fat cow!" she yelled.

The sinister bubble had now grown big enough to engulf all of them. All four began yelling at one another, getting nastier and more aggressive by the second. Even the normally passive Marcus had adopted an overtly bullish stance, his face so close to the fat woman's that they could have smelled each other's breath. I was stupefied by panic when I saw the maroon cloud expand towards me. Even though I could see it, I didn't know how to stop it. I tried to back away but it was too late.

It entered my system through my stomach, which flipped as it did so. I felt my blood rush through my body more quickly, powered on by rage. Heart thudding, cheeks flushing, head throbbing, I let it flow through me and enjoyed the momentary feeling of complete empowerment. Then it flowed out of my throat as a torrent of verbal abuse. I was no longer Genevieve Kelly but a bystander to the spectacle before me. I watched the expletives leave my mouth in physical form, amused as they sank into the cloud and made it grow bigger. One of them hit the woman really hard between the breasts and her voice cracked. She broke down in tears.

In an instant the anger dissipated and we were left in the street, five ordinary people, panting with the effort and relief from the strain of arguing. Marcus even rubbed his eyes as though he were waking up from sleep. I watched the woman being led away by her daughter. Something in their body language betrayed an underlying heartbreak that I had now added to. I was flooded with remorse as I watched them, the woman so grieved that she was now leaning on her daughter for support.

What did I say? Something I said upset her soul. I wish I could say sorry to her.

"Come on, Genevieve. What are you standing there for?" asked Marcus.

"I think I should say sorry."

"Are you thick or something?" asked Vanessa. "What have you got to apologise for?"

"Making her cry. Don't you feel bad?" I asked.

"No," she said decisively.

I studied both their faces for any hint of remorse but found none. We walked home the long way, through Stanmore and down Marsh Lane, probably to work off some of the anger that had stayed behind. As Marcus and Vanessa continued to fight over the last cigarette, I looked to the trees for some kind of salvation but found none.

My grandmother did not have a conventional dining table. Instead she had a wooden picnic table with attached benches, the type that are scattered around parks and in pub gardens. Every year, just as spring would spill into summer, she would hire a handyman to drag it outside. I offered to do it myself but she wouldn't hear of it.

"Ladies should never do a man's work, darling. It shows stupidity, not independence. Why break your back? Surely a woman's looks should be her best investment. If you don't have the money to hire somebody, bake them a cake."

Her eccentricity brought a smile to my face on several occasions. She was wonderful and I thanked Heaven every day for bringing her back to me. I could not talk to her about everything, but there was something about her that made me see everything for what it really was. She seemed to pick up even the tiniest thought pattern and the madness in her method put everything into perspective, whether trivial or serious.

I watched as she stuck the serving spoon in the lasagne. It made a faint squelching sound before hitting the bottom of the Pyrex dish. My grandmother's lasagnes were funny inventions; there was no meat between the pasta sheets, just tomatoes, cheese and peas.

Maybe one of my uncles hated meat as a child so she omitted it. It wouldn't be Dad - he loves the stuff. Or maybe she likes it this way. I wonder what made her reinvent it. Tomatoes contain lycopene, an anti-ageing compound.

I came back to earth when I realised she'd been talking to me for the last five minutes and I had no idea what she'd said. She tossed the salad with frail arms. She had begun to look different and it worried me. Her luminosity had disappeared and her bubble seemed faded and dull. It did not touch the ground any more like everybody else's and the colours had faded to mere shadows of their former selves, particularly towards the lower part of her body. All her movements were a touch unsteady although she was as witty and charismatic as ever. Today, she looked her age.

When I couldn't look at her any more, I dropped my gaze to my lasagne. She had lovingly given me the part with the most cheese. Cheese gave me really bad gas, coupled with gut cramps. *This could be the most painful lunch I have ever eaten. Or I could break the land speed record as I fart-propel myself home.* To avoid eating, I began to speak.

"Grandma, what's wrong with me? Mum keeps taking me to doctors."

"Darling, there's nothing wrong with you other than your dreadful dress sense. Sherry with your lunch or after?"

"Neither thanks. Why did you wait until I was thirteen to make contact? Marcus and Vanessa saw you regularly until I came along." There was a brief pause during which we looked at one another across the table without blinking. I knew that she knew more than she was letting on. She was the first to look away.

"Look, I promised not to utter a word as long as I am alive," she said, then smiled unexpectedly as she went on, "but nobody can silence the old lady once she's gone so I promise that you will find out."

I must have looked horrified.

"Don't you worry, it's nothing sinister or government-related. Just have faith that your grandmother knows everything, she's protecting you and she has her own ways of doing everything." She winked at me with heavily made up eyes and poured me a glass of sherry. I gulped it down without taking my eyes off her.

The rest of the afternoon passed by, warm and fuzzy. Sherry was too sweet for my liking so I was introduced to sparkling wine and cassis instead. It was like an alcoholic Ribena and made me as pissed as a newt for an hour or so. At four o'clock Grandma jumped up, slapped me a few times, sprayed me with lavender water, shoved a mint in my mouth and pushed me out of the door. I staggered to the corner and sat on the low wall behind somebody's hedge. The alcohol had given me a cramp in my calf and as I bent down to massage it I happened to glance back at my grandmother's door. Marcus was making his way up the garden path with the large black bag he normally took to work with him.

I thought he was at work today. He made a real point of telling everyone that this morning. I didn't even know he visited Grandma. How bizarre.

As he reached the front door and raised his fist to knock, it swung open and an old bejewelled hand reached out, grabbed his lapels and pulled him in.

The rain was beating against my window on what might have been the greyest day of the decade. It came in spurts as the wind carried each droplet askew, hurling them like a miniature hand grenades. Between spurts I could see the clouds in the sky, each layer of grey becoming progressively darker towards Earth. Yesterday had been just as miserable. In fact the whole weekend had been a washout. I was waiting for the point when frustration would win me over and I would begin to pace and groan like a caged animal. It didn't come. Instead, I found a new sense of calm watching the sheets of rainwater wash over the urban jungle outside. I amused myself by thinking of it as a kind of celestial payback over those who had the audacity to claim control over nature. *Nature will always win because she's got the knowledge of millennia, whereas we just think we do.*

I caught sight of a reflection in the glass. There was a woman standing behind me, watching me with affection. I sensed that she would not hurt me in any way and that she was not physically there. Her appearance didn't surprise me as nothing surprised me anymore; had I turned around, she would have disappeared so I smiled at her reflection and she smiled back. She was surrounded by pink light and had long hair that merged with the light around her head. Like a popped bubble, she disappeared as suddenly as she had appeared, leaving no trace.

Propping my forehead against the window, I breathed onto the glass until it steamed up around my face. As the rain drummed onto the other side, I held my breath and watched the condensation contract until it vanished altogether. Soon I was asleep.

The nightmare was terrible and it recurred for several weeks thereafter.

I am running away from someone. There is a woman a few paces ahead of me, urging me to hurry up. She is sweating and bleeding from a large open wound in her left arm. One or two drops of blood are blown onto my face as I run behind her but I cannot wipe them off as my arms are trying to propel me forwards. We run across a dual carriageway. Car horns blare from all directions. My heart is pounding, my throat is burning. We run up a steep slope and through trees. I can taste blood in my throat and my legs are ready to give up. I want to stop but I cannot. My will to survive is too strong and urges my body to keep going just that little bit further. I can hear footsteps thudding behind me now.

Gunshots. Someone cries out. I keep running. I reach a fence and climb it without stopping to think, tearing over the barbed wire at the top. I jump over the low wall and run into a multi-storey car park. Somebody grabs me and pulls me down behind a vehicle, putting a hand over my mouth. It smells of sweat and blood. I recognise the ring on the middle finger – it's the woman with the damaged arm.

As the footsteps get closer and slow down, we dart out from our shelter and run towards the stairwell. It's locked. We run up the steep slope to the next floor and the next, without considering where it will lead us. As we get to the top we slow down. There are several armed men standing by a parked van with guns trained on us. A sack is put over my face and I am thrown into the van. I can smell blood again. Then there is silence.

I woke up with a jerk. Breathing heavily, I waited for the feeling of disorientation to pass before I went downstairs and picked up the 'phone. *I need comfort, fast.* I dialled Joe's number.

I was the only Kelly child who had not been barred from Tesco. Marcus had been disallowed at fourteen for having a food fight with his friend Tony and Vanessa had had a cat fight with a thirty year old single mother who, she claimed, had run over her foot with a trolley. Both times, Dad had had to grovel and beg the store manager not to press charges, turning as red as his Irish skin would allow. Then when I was fourteen, I followed in the footsteps of my older siblings, scoring a hat trick for the family.

Crowded places had become increasingly unbearable, especially

Brent Park Tesco. They were a melting pot of bad health, misery and voices that only I could hear. Often I found myself fainting or vomiting before I even walked in. What astounded me more than the Tesco effect was Mum's oblivion to it. Dad said nothing either but stopped asking me to join them once I was old enough to be left at home with Vanessa.

However, this time I was forced to go. Dad was in Ireland visiting relatives and Mum didn't want to go on her own. She had a habit of buying household necessities in bulk, especially toilet paper, and needed assistance carrying her loads to and from the car.

"Genevieve, please come and help," she pleaded. Even with a furrowed brow my mother was very pretty. Her tone was irritating, though.

"No. Take Marcus."

"What? Marcus?" asked a sleepy, half-naked Marcus, stumbling into the kitchen. Mum tutted under her breath.

"You're going to Tesco's with Mum," I said.

"I've been banned. Shame that."

"That was years ago. Don't shave and they won't recognise you."

"Good idea, Genevieve!" cried Mum. She had missed the sarcasm and was genuinely impressed. I grimaced.

"You two can come and help me," Mum said, turning Marcus around and forcing him out of the kitchen and down the hallway towards the stairs. "Don't shave, wear sunglasses," she ordered as Marcus closed his bedroom door.

Twenty minutes later we were hurtling down the A406. Mum was humming to the song in her head and Marcus was fuming beneath the dark glasses, looking more like a rock star with a hangover than someone under cover. The dread of what I could encounter at Tesco was making me feel drained and Marcus' irritation was not allowing me to relax. I shifted in my seat but could not find a position comfortable enough to hold.

"Stop it, Genevieve. Mum's driving," said Marcus sternly. He kept his eyes focussed ahead of him.

"Stop what?"

"Moving. It's pissing me off."

I looked at Mum. She said nothing. She stopped humming though.

He said 'pissing' in front of her. If that had been me, I'd have got a bollocking. Double standards! I continued to fidget.

"If you don't stop," yelled Marcus, "I'm going to beat you up when we get there!"

"I'll beat you back, you big thug!"

"And I," screamed Mum, "will spank you two in public!" That shut us up. Then it made us laugh. Mum didn't see the joke. "Why are you two laughing?"

I stopped laughing when we parked up. Marcus went to get a trolley and Mum made me hold her bag while she fished the shopping list out of her pocket. I noticed that Marcus had two different trainers on. He caught me staring at them.

"Don't ask," he said.

"Okay."

I braced myself as the revolving door swallowed us up and spat us out into the store. The static started in my ears. I walked closely behind my mother for protection but it didn't help. As a reflex I took her arm but that seemed to annoy her. Her bubble grew thick and pushed me away.

"Genevieve, go and get carrots for me. There – look, there."

She pointed and I reluctantly took a step in the direction of her finger. A man was standing by the carrots. He frightened me as my gut recognised him as danger. His small demonic face and beady eyes were fixated on me, his prey. A tiny tongue slithered across his lips as he walked towards me. I closed my eyes, rooted to the spot with fear. As he passed, his shoulder knocked mine, taking a huge chunk of light from my bubble. I felt somebody touching my crotch. A few feet away a man surrounded by grey was looking at me with his head cocked to one side. Long, slippery tentacles were emanating from him and fondling the breasts and private areas of several women in close proximity. I hid behind Marcus as I watched the man go about his business of reading tin labels while he molested people with his thoughts.

"What are you doing, little shitster?" asked Marcus, gently taking my head in a mock headlock.

"Marcus, that man…"

"Did he do something? He looks odd."

Marcus pushed his sunglasses onto his head and took a step in the direction of the man. He walked off, leaving me feeling physically sick and violated. The static noises turned to screeching and I looked around for the source. It was coming from everywhere.

Ooo, nice buns on that guy.

Bitch left me with nothing. I hate women.

I'm so tired this morning, too much booze, not enough sleep again.

Why am I fat? Whatever I eat just sits on my hips. I hate my body.

Wish I'd never married. Hope he dies in his sleep.

Calories aren't in celery are they?

If I put this in my handbag who'll see?

Two hundred grammes will cost forty pence…

My head began to hurt and I felt my sweater become wet around the collar.

"Jesus!" exclaimed Marcus, cupping my face with his sleeve. My nose was bleeding profusely, running down my chin in a double rivulet and creating a red bib on my sweater.

"Madam, can I ask you to come with me? You're putting customers off buying," said a middle-aged man in a Tesco uniform. He beckoned for me to follow him.

"Are you serious?" asked Marcus.

He took his hand away for a second. The sudden inhalation of putrid air was all I needed to cover the potatoes in vomit. The man looked at the potatoes in horror. My head began to throb but I heard every thought.

Disgusting child. Ought to be sold or strangled. Look at her retching and bleeding like that. All children should be beaten senseless and locked up.

"If you don't like kids then don't work in a public place," I said, annoyed that my voice sounded so pathetic.

"Your mother's done a terrible job," he said curtly.

"Don't bring my mother into this, you turd," I said. His hatred was catching on like an infectious disease.

"And your boyfriend isn't much better. Looks like he didn't even wash this morning."

"You sound like you didn't get enough sleep last night," I retorted.

Mum had hurried over after noticing the blood on my face. She didn't say a word but looked at me from every angle to make sure I had no open wounds.

"Madam, is this your daughter?" asked an acne-ridden man in his thirties.

"Yes," replied my mother.

"I'm afraid you'll have to pay for the damage."

"What damage?" asked Marcus and Mum together, equally outraged.

"The vegetables," he said softly but sternly, gesturing at the vomit-covered potatoes.

"Hey, hey, hey, my sister," said Marcus, articulating the word 'sister' in the direction of the uniformed man, "was sick. She didn't do it on purpose."

The man's bubble became black and cloudy like smog as Marcus began to argue with the store manager about his conduct. The static became overridden by low-pitched groaning and I was desperate to leave. I didn't want to be sick again but I had to do something to break the flow of argument and leave before the man's loathing engulfed me and buried me alive. When I could bear it no longer I picked up an onion, threw it at the man and fled; it hit him square in the face and bounced off. The security guard at the door scooped me up as I ran past. I fainted as he caught me and my nosebleed started again.

Back at home, Marcus was the only sympathiser. Mum was not speaking to me and after hearing what had happened from Mum, Vanessa decided to give me the silent treatment too. I didn't care. I missed Dad terribly. He acted as a buffer behind which I could sit in security. My head still felt fuzzy and my stomach and throat throbbed strangely as I lay listlessly on the sofa for the rest of the day.

Dad called later in the evening, asking for me specifically. Mum must have already told him what had happened because it was unlike Dad not to speak to her first.

"Evening, Tiger. Marcus tells me you were sick today. That true?"

"You sound more Irish today," I said before pausing to blink back my tears. "I puked on the potatoes."

"Everything okay at school? You aren't worried about any-thing are you?"

"School's fine. Mum's not talking to me. I think she's peeved. I didn't do it on purpose." I began to cry silently. Dad must have noticed because his voice softened further until it was barely more than a whisper.

"She's just in shock, Tiger. She got scared. I would have too if I'd seen you puke all over the potatoes. Being Irish, that would have frightened me more than you know!" He laughed at his own joke. "Seriously, Tiger. You're my little cub remember? And I've got a surprise just for you…"

The 'phone crackled and scraped before giving me a nervous "Hello?"

"Grandma!"

"Yes darling, it's me. Don't go into public places like that.

They're full of miserable, grotty people who can't see the best in anything or be happy for anyone. Stay away from people with bad thoughts." Whispering into the receiver, she continued, "And don't worry about your mother. She'll never see what you do."

"Never?"

"No, but you'll come across different people, it's a part of life. Just don't do things you aren't comfortable with. Genevieve, I promise you, it may not seem this way, but you are blessed."

"Okay, Grandma."

A large lump formed in my throat as I put the receiver back on its cradle. There was no time to honour my feeling of loneliness, however, as Marcus breezed in with a video cassette and a box of spicy potato wedges.

"Got some potatoes you won't puke over!" he announced and threw the box into my lap.

The trepidation was almost too great to bear. As I crouched alone behind the trees, I thought of all the times Daniella and Philip had hurt me. The autumnal breeze was cool and refreshing, lifting my hair and stroking my face as if to get my attention and reason with me. Ten years of abuse was finally about to end. I was going to put a stop to it. Unable to go anywhere without being chaperoned had brought me to the end of my tether.

I remembered how Daniella and Philip had systematically destroyed my school experience from the very beginning. Horrible images flashed through my mind: PE bag swung in face, aged five; fingers smacked with ruler, aged eight; hair chopped off, aged…

A deep, dark rage had fermented within me for a decade now. It simmered beneath the calm, quiet surface, about to be given an outlet. I began to feel excitement, nervous, wonderful excitement, touched by the promise of redemption. I had planned this. From the moment I had set foot in that martial arts class six years ago I had envisaged this moment; the culmination of everything I had learned. It had been a wonderful means to this end. The discipline was apt and a stark contrast to the bullying tactics adopted by my foe. I just prayed that they would understand the irony one day.

Earlier that day, Daniella had broken the Parker pen that my grandmother had given me for my fourteenth birthday. She had held it to my jugular, threatened to slit my throat with it before abruptly turning and hurling it like a dart at an invisible dartboard. The crack of the broken nib had echoed in the empty classroom, a repetitive reminder of shattered sentiment. I had done nothing but watch her cackle with piggy eyes flashing simultaneous nervousness and pathetic achievement. Retaliation would not have worked in my favour then. Instead, I stared long and hard at the teeth I would knock out later. No sense of failure crossed my mind after that. I was far too angry and my anger was an assurance of success.

Daniella and Philip ambled through the entrance of Camrose Park. I observed them, fat blobs rippling with every heavy foot-step. Their limp hair and rough features would never allow them to appear as anything other than unkempt. A big dark cloud of rage rose up from my chest, momentarily obscuring my field of vision. I took a deep breath.

Calm down and concentrate, Genevieve. You're supposed to be launching a pre-emptive strike, remember? Think, they'll never have what you have. Maybe they know it. It's certainly obvious to you. They disgust you.

The twins moved like a wall, the front advancing in natural synchronisation. A flash of pity swept through my senses. Their aggression was a mask for their ignorance and mediocrity. In this world designed to force us to use our individual talents to survive, they had none. No wonder they were so aggressive. Ruthless and beyond the point of no return, I determined to exploit their weakness.

174

The car park and allotments were empty. There was nobody in sight. *Perfect.*

I had wrapped old handkerchiefs around my knuckles just in case contact with the twins would give me a disease. Lately my revulsion of dirt had got worse and had started to include people, not just pavements and surfaces. *I have no intention of letting the germs of those two slugs ruin my skin, contaminate my blood or cause failure in my internal organs. God knows what's been breeding on them. Ugh!*

As they approached, my heart began to beat louder but not faster. I was overcome by a strange sense of calm and protection. Justice was going to be meted out today, one way or another. The feeling of flow took over the situation.

I stepped out into their path with my hands behind my back. Every muscle was tensed, tightly coiled and under my control. They both snorted with laughter but stopped abruptly when their bubbles came into contact with mine. Daniella began to speak but didn't get a chance to. The moment I saw her mouth open, I threw my fist into it, ten years of resentment and rage powering it. When she opened her mouth again, blood spilled out. Philip had ducked and crouched on the ground, knowing that he was too heavy to outrun me. I waited for him to get up and when he did my boot forced a dent in his belly, knocking the wind out of him and cracking his ribs. To this day I can remember the awful sensation of that hollow, wooden snap. I shuddered and looked down at Philip, watching him writhe on the floor for a moment. Daniella had already picked up her teeth and waddled off, leaving her brother to his fate.

"I... I'm... sorry," he puffed, as he clutched his enormous abdomen. I acknowledged the look of understanding on his face. He knew exactly what he was apologising for.

I turned and walked away as calmly as though I had seen nothing out of the ordinary occur. A smile of relief melted the tension from my face. I felt a small explosion in my back as a lifelong block of energy dissipated and then my back muscles loosened, making me feel noticeably taller. A weight had been lifted. I stood behind the pavilion as I removed the bandages from my knuckles and let the fresh air fill my lungs. Philip was hobbling out of the park, doubled over, clearly in agony. I felt nothing. The smile on my face grew until it reached the tips of my fingers and toes.

As I made my way down the path towards home, I could sense someone walking with me to my right. I turned a full three-hundred and sixty degrees. All that stirred around me were the leaves, brought to life by the breeze.

NINE

Diagnosis

I should probably have died, becoming an additional member of the ethereal Davis family and one more virtual assistant for Matthew.

Michael Davis wanted to speak with me. He had waited in the doorway of the lounge until I came home from school. He was the first thing I saw as I pushed open the front door, beckoning for me to come in and join him in the living room. As I made myself comfortable, he lit his pipe with the usual familiarity and shook it gently. I watched him with vague amusement as he hitched up his trousers and squatted in front of the fireplace, lighting the fire and stoking it with a large iron rod. Only my conscience prevented my inner devil from asking him why he had started a fire in midsummer, after watching him complete the task. I liked Michael Davis and I would rather sweat to death than inconvenience him.

We smiled at each other warmly as he sat down in his usual chair and crossed his legs. The smoke from his pipe had begun to tickle my nostrils and I sneezed several times. He put his pipe down on a side table and rested his arms along the armrests of his chair. He didn't display any nervous ticks or fidget in the slightest, something I noticed immediately and admired greatly.

I wish I could be so composed. Did he train himself or was he born like that?

Margaret bustled in with a silver tray of tea and an assortment of tiny scones and cakes. I watched as she deftly laid it out on the table without so much as a tinkle or clatter. She was very nimble for a woman so buxom and she had the slim, long fingers of a lady. She smiled at her husband, kissed my forehead and poured out two cups of tea before leaving.

"The secret to a very happy marriage is for each partner to respect that the other likes to do things their own way. If I had told my wife what to do and how to do it, this home would not be so well organised or comfortable. I'm dreadful at organising anything."

"If you don't mind me asking, do you ever argue?" I asked.

"Yes. If a couple didn't argue there would be something seriously wrong. Genevieve, all relationships are based on two or more individuals with their own ways and their own opinions. Margie and I disagree, yes, but we talk issues through."

"Who has the final say?"

"I do, with Margie's permission." He winked.

"You wanted to see me about something specific?" I asked.

He nodded in affirmation as he tapped his pipe on the table top.

"Genevieve, dear, we must discuss what you are to do with your future."

I hesitated. As a rule, I didn't discuss my dreams and aspirations with anybody, bar Joe. Yet, here I was, feeling obliged to open my heart to a ghost, a genuine ethereal entity. I wasn't sure what my next move should be so I waited for Michael Davis to speak again.

"You seem reluctant," he said at length.

"Well, I'm not entirely sure what to say. I haven't really thought about it yet."

That was a blatant lie and my lack of eye contact must have exposed me. Since I was a child I had wanted to travel around the world to exotic places, observing people, tasting foods, blending into a variety of backgrounds.

"You have."

"Well, and I do mean this with all due respect, things have changed since your day. I do want to get married and settle down, but there's so much to do first. I mean … " I sighed when I realised that I couldn't find the words to express what I wanted to say. Michael Davis looked directly into my eyes.

"Actually, I was going to suggest that you travel abroad."

For the next hour or so Michael Davis took me on a magical verbal tour of all the different places he had worked. We discussed his wonderful assortment of souvenirs and native artefacts, my various options and even finances. The finer points of our talk are something I have always kept to myself, as my secret. Several decisions were made in that hour that determined my journey for the rest of my life, their repercussions spreading through the years like ripples through water.

It was bitterly cold in the stables. I was wearing Marcus's old BMX gloves but the cold was seeping through the padding and cutting off my circulation. I recalled a few winters ago when our school was closed due to burst water pipes. *Oh God, sorry for taking your name in vain, but I wonder if the same thing happens to blood vessels. If mine all burst I wouldn't be able to wipe up the mess.* The thought of my fingers exploding caused me to shiver more violently so I wedged my hands in my armpits and stamped.

"Genevieve, stop that." Matthew was annoyed.

"Sorry. I'm cold and my feet are freezing."

"Relieve yourself on them when they go blue."

"Yuck! Stamping is more my style."

"If the horse is startled, he'll kick me and then I'll kick you."

Matthew did not look up but I could tell by his tone that he was serious. He had become engrossed in the delicate task he was performing. I was not sure what that was but it had something to do with the horse he noticed had been limping earlier. He finished and let the horse's hoof down gently.

"Don't you feel dizzy when you suddenly straighten up like that?" I asked.

"No."

"I do."

"No meat, fussy eater, not enough blood and strength."

No eye contact, minimal words used, not enough sleep. I became surprised at my own irritation. *Must be about to start my period.*

"Matthew, can I ask you something?"

He stopped and leaned on the bottom half of the stable door.

"You will anyway."

"It's a bit rude though, Matthew."

"No."

"Please."

"No."

"I don't know who else to ask."

"No."

"But I thought you of all people might know about these things. I'm getting really frustrated with it."

"Genevieve," he said, bending down so that our eyes were level, "there are certain things a lady should only do once she's married." I burst out laughing.

"No, it's got nothing to do with that."

"Then what?"

If Matthew's face had allowed it, confusion would have

washed over his features at that moment. Instead he straightened his back and waited, as still as a statue, until I had finished laughing. He waited a long time.

"Why would you put the word 'arse' on a jar label?" I asked.

No doubt Matthew's face would have shown even more confusion at this point because several minutes passed before he stirred. I began to wonder if he'd lost patience with me.

"Pardon?" he asked. His tone betrayed a hint of shock.

"I've seen a jar with the word 'arse' written on it. Knowing what an uptight witch the owner is, it can't be a joke. She doesn't have a sense of humour. What could it stand for?" For the first time since we'd met, Matthew raised his eyebrows. Also for the first time since we'd met, his expression softened a little.

"Know how ladies older than yourself keep their skin so white?"

"No."

"Then you've been spending far too long outdoors with me," he snapped.

It was my turn to be confused now. As I struggled with Matthew's cryptic answer, he vanished, and I was left outside the dilapidated shell of the stables in twentieth century Canons Park with nobody but a crow for company.

Normally, I did not venture uphill beyond Stoney Fields. There was something about that area that made me uneasy. I didn't want to discover what was so sinister about it for fear that it would be even more unsavoury than Honeypot Lane. My gut reaction was different too – rather than feel queasy, I could almost hear an internal alarm go off in the bottom of my stomach.

I managed to avoid the area until the summer of 1994. Dad had been building a new shed and generally revamping the garden. As I had finished my GCSEs the week before, he had enlisted my help for holding planks in place while he measured, drew, sawed and banged. John Graham would patiently sit by the rose bushes watching us, sometimes cocking his head to one side in curiosity at Dad's power tools. In the evenings I was free to do what I wanted as Marcus was home to help. Joe was often waiting for me at the entrance to Edgware station. We would take the first bus that arrived and explore wherever it took us.

The third Friday in July was warm and sunny. Mum woke me up early and gave me a list of errands to run.

"Wha…? Can't V'nessa do it?" I moaned, eyes still closed and mouth half paralysed with sleep.

"Because she has a shoot on Tuesday and needs her beauty sleep."

I didn't want to argue with Mum so I peeled my eyes open to take a look at her list. Number three was 'Give umbrella back to Aunty Gina'.

"Oh bloody bugger it!" I groaned. "She lives up in bloody no-where beyond bloody Broadfields."

I took ages in the bathroom, put on my clothes as slowly as I could and brushed each individual hair on my head. I was hoping that if I took long enough to get ready, Mum would either think I was ill or lose patience and go herself. My lack of effort was in vain. She was in an uncharacteristically chirpy mood and even gave me a kiss before pushing me out of the front door. I managed to grimace at her for effect before she shut it behind me. I sighed and dragged my Doc Martened feet to the bus station to look at the map of Edgware displayed on the wall. Hopefully, I could take a new and longer route to Gina's. My gut feeling was right; unless I wanted to spend the whole day getting there I would have to walk through Broadfields.

Fanbloodytastic! I don't even like Gina. She checks my hair for nits every time she sees me and asks if I've started my period.

As expected, the leaden feeling started in my legs half way up

Edgwarebury Lane. As I crossed the bridge over the Watford Bypass, my skin began to crawl and my breathing grew rapid and shallow. By the time I had passed Wolmer Close, I was sweating so profusely that I had to stop and fan myself with the umbrella.

This is sinister. I can feel the fear here and I don't want to know why.

When I looked up, I was not surprised to see that the road and houses had completely disappeared and I was standing in a field scattered with small huts. A few hundred metres away was a walled enclosure. A lot of yelling and crying came from within, along with other noises.

"It's a prison, lady," said a voice in my left ear.

I turned round but there was nobody there. This was strange and new to me. I had never been able to hear someone so clearly without being able to see them. Being curious and young, I decided to investigate the prison but I was stopped by a physical obstacle - my legs were refusing to move.

"It's dangerous. People are tortured and starved and left to die in disease there."

Once again, there was nobody there. My legs could not move forward, almost as if they were jammed tight against a wall. I could smell male body odour but couldn't catch sight of anyone no matter how quickly I turned around.

"Lady, they are entertainment or target practice for the soldiers."

"Why?"

"They don't want their governance or just can't pay the taxes."

I took a step back and felt some relief from the tightness that had been gripping my abdomen.

"Who are you?" I asked loudly.

Nothing.

"Hello?"

Nothing.

I looked down when I felt myself sink a little. I was standing on a dirt track and decided to follow it. Part of it ran alongside a small stream that glistened in the morning sun and looked very pretty, like a postcard but with an extra dimension of beauty that could not be captured by a camera. The settlement of Edgware looked like a cluster of dots in the distance. Just at the moment when my belly grumbled its first request for food, I spotted another walled enclosure but this time it was immense. I saw that it was heavily guarded by Roman soldiers.

Other than those on active sentry duty, there were groups of them mending sandals and spears. The gates were wide open and the scent of fresh bread wafted out of them, into my nostrils and hit my brain.

I caught the eye of one the soldiers and he strolled towards me. Instantly, I knew something was not right and backed away. It could have been the way he looked me up and down, the way he licked his lips as he came closer or the way he laughed without taking his eyes off me when I threw the umbrella at him. Screaming for help, I turned and ran for my life.

I didn't see the car that hit me. Fortunately, I don't remember much about the accident at all. What I do clearly recall is running away from a Roman soldier and waking up four days later to the most excruciating pain I could ever imagine. This time I did not escape with a few bruises and a headache. The impact had tossed me up in the air like a rag-doll, bringing me down limp and broken onto the roof of the car behind the one that hit me. My right leg had been swept from under me and hit my left leg so hard that the patella broke clean in half. As I came down onto the roof, the pen in my pocket had impaled my left arm, and my ribcage had splintered, piercing my lungs and leaving me to drown in my own blood. I had coughed and spluttered, watching the ballpoint protruding from my bicep gradually fade into black. Had I not been a stone's throw from the Royal National Orthopaedic

Hospital I should probably have died, becoming an additional member of the ethereal Davis family and one more virtual assistant for Matthew.

So what should have been the best summer of my life ended up being the one I have most difficulty remembering. The pain put a prism around me, one where every side demonstrated a different form of it: sharp, throbbing, tearing, bruised. Sometimes I would wake up to find Joe sitting beside me, his chocolate eyes huge with worry.

What time is it Joe? Is it daylight outside? Where are my parents?

Sometimes when the pain was too great and my mouth too dry to articulate words, I would think them, will them to Joe, hoping that he would catch them from the ether and answer me. But he could only sense my dry mouth and would insert a straw through my lips, coaxing me to drink as he stroked my hair. Joe exhibited a tenderness rare at our age, I suppose, but as I watched him watch me I wondered whether this was how he would be with me twenty, thirty, fifty years from now. The thought helped me heal.

Mum and Dad did not spend as much time at my bedside as one might think a worried parent should. This was not because they were fed up or had given up on me. The hospital had looked at my previous medical records and called in Social Services to investigate. My parents were subjected to what my mother called "An absolutely humiliating witch hunt in which your parents were assumed guilty before being proved otherwise. The shame of it." Seeing my parents so frightened and confused made me decide, once and for all, to do whatever it took to become 'normal' again. Whatever that was.

I do not recall the interviews, examinations and tests that filled up the five weeks of my hospital stay. I do not even remember my consultant's name, although his voice is as clear as a bell inside my head and if I close my eyes it is as though he is here in the room with me. What I do remember is leaving hospital with a diagnosis of schizophrenia and returning home to find that Vanessa had gone for good.

Vanessa's bedroom had a life of its own. I had very rarely ventured in there other than to put clean laundry on her bed or switch the boiler on. When we had first moved, I hadn't paid much attention to her room, thinking it was Vanessa that had made me feel the discomfort. Once I had passed through puberty, though, the life force of the room opened up to me, trying to grab me at every opportunity, becoming angry with me every time it failed. Walking into it could only be compared to walking into a dark cave that never ended. Even during daylight, it was dark and dull, with no concept of time. It was the boiler that I feared most. I could hear it breathing in the darkness like a predatory animal, trapped in its cage of semi-death. Sometimes it would cry tears of such sorrow that I would begin to cry too.

Eventually I had stopped going in. I was used to having cold showers. Still, every time I had walked past the door, I couldn't help but look in and wonder who the room really belonged to.

The Artex ceiling in the room was dead. Even though I had been staring at it, it did not come to life and dance its seductive hula in front of my eyes. I wanted it to so badly but the drugs had put treacle in my head and all I could see was death. It was all alien to me and I was too desensitised to be frightened now.

Nothing's fluid anymore.

I looked at Vanessa's desk by her window. Normally there would be the old imprint of her after she had got up from the chair or wisps of spent anger after she had lost her temper and thrown something. Even the window looked dull and lifeless. I couldn't see the movement of sunlight at all. *Is this what hell looks like?*

It was not just my brain that had slowed down. My metabolism must have too because I had finally managed to put on some weight. I looked down my nose at the two new mounds on my chest.

Boobs! Welcome!

Downstairs, Mum and Dad were having another row. It was my fault again. I could hear them but by the time the words hit the right path to my brain, the thought had already passed. My mind was too foggy to register such processes and I was completely desensitised to the accompanying emotion. Not only was there treacle in my head but I had been wrapped up in invisible bubble wrap. My supposed friends, the drugs, had created a buffer zone between myself and the world around me, trapping in my own personal ghetto. Neither education nor a good job could get me out.

Marcus is in Lanzarote.

For some reason I found that funny and giggled maniacally. I lay back on the bed and stared at the ceiling again. My head was empty for the most part now. Even the commotion downstairs could not fill it up.

"She's not herself, Eloise, look at her!"

The quilt is white and fluffy.

"But she's better now. See how normal she is? No more talking to imaginary friends."

"She's lost her spark! I want my daughter back the way she was. She's not schizo, she's just more intelligent than most. I wish you'd recognise that for once!"

"No! She seems better to me."

"No more drugs and doctors, I'm warning you!"

"She needs medicating."

"What? She's already doing badly at school!"

"Rubbish! She's got good grades."

"Not this term, she hasn't."

Maybe it's snow.

"I'll leave you, so help me! I'll take my daughter and leave!"

"You can't do that!" Mum wailed really loud.

Let's make snow angels.

I flapped my arms and legs for a bit. The movement was slow. Beneath me the shouting had stopped.

I'll never be bored again, now that I'm stupid.

Dad thundered upstairs, shaking the ground as he stomped. My bedroom door slammed, then the bathroom door. Vanessa's door swung open violently and hit the cupboard next to it. A small sliver of varnish chipped off and slithered onto the floor. I knew Dad was angry but I couldn't feel any of it.

Ah, ignorance really is bliss. Stupidity is bliss.

"Get up, Genevieve!" he roared, throwing my coat at me.

Yep, he's angry. He called me Genevieve.

I arose slowly and put the coat on. It was a little more snug than usual. Dad began to rummage in my pockets. His skin was bright red except around his mouth and eyes. He looked like a psychedelic panda cartoon. I was too dumbed down to ask what he was doing but I didn't have to.

"Where are those goddamn pills? You're not taking them anymore, d'you hear me?"

"Okay."

Dad grabbed my hand and marched me down the stairs. Mum ran down after us and tried to block his path as he put on his shoes.

"Please Padraig," she whimpered, "don't take my daughter away from me. I've already lost one."

"For fuck's sake, Eloise! We're going for an ice cream."

Had I not been in a drug-induced stupor, I would have been stunned. I had never heard Dad swear before and I never would again. He shoved me into the car.

"Dad, where are we going?" I asked. The seat belt clicked neatly into place.

"I don't know."

The rattling of the car going over the cattle grid woke me up. My eyes didn't have to open because I knew exactly where we were.

We had visited Aldenham Country Park almost every other Sunday from birth to adolescence. The ritual had always been the same; we would take a walk through the woods, feed the ducks and swans with the seed Mum bought from the Old Seed Man and then sit on the grass eating our Mr Whippy ice creams or drinking hot chocolate, depending on the weather. As we were in our church attire, Mum would bring plastic bags for us to sit on. After we tired of the park, Dad would drive us up the road to watch the aeroplanes take off at the Elstree aerodrome flying school. We would park outside and peep over the hedge as the engines purred and whirred above us. Until I was old enough to know better, I assumed that all light aircraft made that noise because they were jet-fart propelled by a pilot on a baked beans diet. I loved our Sunday routine, even though it rarely varied. It filled us with excitement and was my only incentive for behaving in church in the morning.

Dad and I strolled slowly through the woodland listening to the crackling twigs beneath our feet. Normally, I would rest my hand in the crook of Dad's elbow as we walked but he was upset today so I didn't. It was a shame I could neither see his anger nor feel it, but familiarity with the lines on his forehead led me to believe he was upset and needed space to ponder.

Is this what other people do – read clues on faces?

"Do you feel any different with these drugs, Tiger?"

"I feel thick."

"You're not doing well at school lately."

That was true. I had done very well in my GCSEs, with eight A grades and a U in Physics. I didn't see the point of Physics so I had simply decided not to devote any time or effort to studying for the papers.

"Dad, I'd rather be considered mad than stupid."

There's nothing more mediocre and insipid than being stupid.

"Well Tiger, you're not to take those pills anymore and that's that. How do you feel?"

"Fat. I feel fat. Like I haven't pooed properly for days even though I have."

"You couldn't be fat if you tried!"

Silence. A squirrel leapt from the branch of one tree onto the branch of another nearby. I watched with interest but could not feel any awe.

Blasted desensitisation. I can't even get annoyed with it.

"You know, Mum means well. She's got a good heart, Tiger. She only wants what's best for you but sometimes she lets her pride and stubbornness get in the way."

"Sometimes?"

"All right, she's always been that way."

"And I thought the stubbornness came from your side of the family."

"That's what all women say. You will too when you have children."

"How did you both meet?"

Until that day I had never been interested in how my parents met. Suddenly, I found myself wanting to know what they were like before having children.

"We took the same Maths module at university. I met your mum at a party there. Didn't bother to ask her out – she was a snooty fashion model in those days and she was clever. Way out of my league. Anyway, my friend Gerry had his eye on her."

"Then what happened?"

"Gerry asked her out but she told him to get lost."

"And then?"

"Well, she cornered me in the cafeteria a few weeks later, really offended that I hadn't noticed some signals she'd been giving off." Dad scratched his head. "Bloody confusing, you women."

"Then?"

"Well, I had to take her out to the summer charity ball."

"And?"

"It was useless! I couldn't understand a word she said with that accent of hers."

"So what happened next?"

"I had to take her out again and again before I could make head or tail of what she was saying. Next thing I knew, we've finished college and got engaged!"

"Oh," I said, as deflated as I could possibly be in that state.

"What?"

"Nothing. I just thought that I must have originated from some type of romance, that's all, especially seeing as Mum's so beautiful."

"Tiger, I'm a man, an engineer at that. I don't understand romance. Call it my personal handicap."

Everything looks so dull. I don't like this. I want to be me again.

Dad was still talking but I was far too busy looking at the world around me. It was new and unfamiliar. I felt uncomfortable. This was the first time I had been outdoors since starting my course of schizophrenia medication. Joe had tried his best to coax me out during the day but I felt bloated and lethargic and had resisted. My discomfort turned to mild incredulity, if you can call it that.

I can't believe people go through life like this. How boring! I'd rather die than spend the rest of my life as one of the living dead.

But within months my confidence had returned, my grades were back to their usual standard and I was weird to the world again. Mum was gentler with me now, although she avoided me whenever she could, working overtime at least four out of five weekdays. She was still terribly hurt that Vanessa has walked out on us the way she did, without so much as a goodbye. The rest of the time she worried about me, in secret, though the furrows between her eyebrows gave her away.

Vanessa had not kept in touch with Mum, Dad or me but I could tell from the way Marcus shifted whenever her name was mentioned that she still kept in touch with him. Sometimes I would talk about her in order to watch him squirm, wanting him to know that I had guessed his dirty secret and would never forgive him for it.

The first part of my seventeenth year was the only one that provided me with a taste of what it was like to be a truly ordinary teenager. From the September after my accident to just after Bonfire Night, I did not see John Graham, Margaret and Michael Davis or Matthew. Evelyn and I did not cross paths either. In fact, I was blissfully oblivious to her sinister presence the whole time. This new-found freedom from the trappings of my own mind gave me the extra time and inclination to reflect on what I really wanted to do. For the first time in my life I felt hopeful about my future and welcomed it. It took a while to get used to this light and happy feeling but, once I did, I embraced it and watched how life reacted positively as the burden lifted. I did miss my ethereal friends but deep down in the pit of my stomach was a feeling that told me that they would be back and that this freedom would not last for much longer.

That November, Joe and I sat down and discussed our dreams as young adults.

"Joe, I want to get out of here. For a while. I know that life will bring me back here, there's no escape. But I want to get away from the judgement, constraints, everything."

"Hopefully, Gen, we'll both go to the same university or at least within driving distance. I've got this car I want to do up. And we can live together, get our own place."

"Yes, my mother would just love that. She's very proud of her selection of meat cleavers too and loves using them. Any kind of meat will do."

"It was just an idea." Joe actually blushed. I had never seen him blush before. That was my forte, whereas Joe didn't feel any shame at all most of the time.

"Why did you blush, Joe?"

"I didn't. I can't. I'm too dark and even if I did, it wouldn't show."

"Rubbish. You're not that dark and you did blush. Why?"

"No, I didn't."

"Why?"

Joe knew that I would keep asking until he gave me a satisfactory answer. Taking a long, deep breath he said, "Well, it's just hit me that we're older now and I know what I want out of life."

"What's that?"

"To settle down with you."

"But, Joe, there's a whole world out there I want to see first. With you."

"Gen, travelling the world isn't easy. We don't have any money for starters and I really want to learn more about physiotherapy, maybe get a good degree and then specialise." He laughed out loud. "And I can't imagine you taking money from your parents."

"No, there are other ways."

"Taking off your gran? That's criminal."

"No, Joe."

That was another one of Joe's foibles and it made me smile inside. He had never met his grandparents but he still had a very deep respect and affection for old people. Animals too. I loved him for it. He hated kids though, which was fine by me.

"Joe, I'm going to make as much money as I can in business this year and invest it wisely."

I was expecting Joe to make fun of my sweeping statement but he didn't. Instead he gave me a hug, a proper grown up hug, without pretending that I stank after letting me go. We were sixteen now so there was no need for that kind of childishness anymore.

"Gen, if I decided to go to university while you travelled, would you still love me? I just want to make sure I can look after you, I guess."

"Of course. We both need to do what's right for us. We'll always end up back here with each other, whatever happens in between. I promise."

"You've always been the go-getter."

"Well, I really enjoyed my little business ventures of yesteryear! And it's something I'm good at."

"You're good at everything and I'm thankful you're with me."

Within weeks I had set up a small, one-woman business venture under my grandmother's name. I hired myself out to paint murals and made artefacts that I sold through word-of-mouth. Those were the days before the Internet revolution but that didn't stop me or slow me down. By the time I had sat my first A Level exam I had almost ten thousand pounds in a high interest savings account and I knew exactly where I was going with it.

TEN

Love And Music

Everything happens for a reason.
I wonder what I'm here for.

Grandma and I walked the short distance from her house to Edgware General Hospital. An old friend of hers had died there years before so she spent every Friday and some Saturdays there helping at the snack shop as a personal thank you. She had moved the seventy-five year old photo of her old school group to the front of the mantelpiece recently as more and more of them had passed away. Decades-old memories had begun to fade or become distorted and it was Grandma's way of keeping them alive and true in her heart. I wondered what it would be like to be old like that and have to look back for the good times rather than forwards to a promising future. I wondered if there was anything Grandma would have changed, any part of her long history that she would have wished to rewrite, given the opportunity.

"My dear, there's just no point in thinking that way," she would laugh at my naivety. "Such regrets only make a person ugly to the outside world. If you have to look back, do so remembering your accomplishments, even if you consider them too small to count."

"Grandma, I really hope and pray that one day I'll be just like you." She recoiled in horror. I saw the way her bubble retreated and turned lumpy, almost as though it had congealed.

"Genevieve, NEVER try to be someone else!"

"But…"

"No buts. Would Joe feel the same if you were somebody different? Ask him why he chose you and not some hair-brained tart."

Joe and I had officially started dating that September and Mum had started watching me like a hawk for signs of pregnancy and other silly ideas that festered in her Catholic mind. My grandmother understood my inclination to be out of her scrutiny as much as possible so she allowed me to accompany her to the hospital every Friday. I had never seen her in a social setting until then, for some reason finding it impossible to imagine her interacting with fellow pensioners. She was far too glamorous. So it was both surprising and heartening to see her fit in so well with all of them, even the dowdy ones. She did stand out though, very colourful and elegant, in contrast to the usual nondescript uniform of pastel cardigans, sensible shoes and A-line skirts.

Until then I had imagined all old people were full of trapped wind and suffered perpetual joint pains. They tended to complain about the same things: their equally old children, Post Office queues, an inability to read the small print on anything official and the crappy excuse for music that young people listened to. Accompanying Grandma to the hospital and meeting more of them I discovered how interesting they truly were and how extraordinary some of their lives had been. I sat on a creaky plastic chair, listening in amusement as they moaned about the rubbish on television nowadays.

"Didn't think you were the type to hang out with geriatrics," Joe teased. He had slipped in quietly and pulled up a chair next to me. I noticed how he was wearing his baggiest tracksuit bottoms to cover his modesty and avoid the hullabaloo of the previous week when he'd come in wearing his football shorts and caused all the old ladies to suffer palpitations and hot flushes at the sight of his tanned legs. Two had asked him to dance the tango and one had offered to sit on his lap and keep him warm. Not that I was jealous in the slightest. He had looked mortified though. As he now took charge of stacking the chairs and collecting stray magazines, Grandma took me aside.

"Darling, I want you to miss your judo class tomorrow and come to see me."

"Tae Kwon Do. But I'm not going until my legs have fully healed. Is everything okay?"

"Yes, but there's something I want to show you. Don't bring Casanova, will you," she said, nodding at Joe. I blushed furiously. "I'll see you at nine-thirty. Bert, the old RAF mechanic, is going to give me a lift home. You know, that Bert. So you two lovers can enjoy each other's company all the way home."

I could feel my cheeks burning.

"Are you feeling hot?" Joe asked looking a bit concerned.

"She is, dear, but not in the way you think."

Oh how I wish the ground would swallow me up right now. I waved goodbye to Grandma and Bert. The fog of confusion was hovering around Joe's head again.

Thank God men are a bit dafter than women in some respects. It's saved me a lot of embarrassment. Still, it's one of the things that make me so proud of her. She really did break the mould.

I looked at Joe, my Joe, with his slightly overgrown hair and his coffee-coloured skin. He was at his most handsome caught off-guard, when the light ran down the sides of his face and freeze-framed it for a split second. Whenever he looked directly at me I would get lost as if nothing else existed other than the comforting brown of his eyes and the thud-thud-thud of my heart. We were as one all the way home, cocooned in the same protective bubble, so tightly tied together by intertwining heart strings that it was physically painful when we were forced to bid each other farewell. We took our time walking home in the yellow light of the street-lamps, hand in hand, talking about nothing in particular. It was nine-thirty when I got home, by which time Mum was threatening to lock me in my room indefinitely and chop Joe's bits off. I was too blissfully happy to hear a word she said.

Grandma was at her carefree best the next morning, having risen at six o'clock to bake teacakes for me. I had arrived early enough to catch her without her 'face' on. Even with the deep wrinkles on her forehead and around her eyes, she still looked incredibly attractive. I watched as she painted a masterpiece of camouflage on her face. She treated it as a canvas - prepping, patting and stroking every last detail of feminine deception. I thought of my own routine of moisturiser and a quick hair brush-ing with a touch of shame. Admittedly, puberty had not ravaged my skin and hair like most of the other kids at school. I still had skin like a baby's backside and Joe loved to touch it. Nothing else seemed important to me.

"Darling, I'm going to take you make-up shopping for Christmas. You must start using Yardley. Are you going to France this year?"

"Not sure yet."

"Why don't you spend Christmas with me? We've never seen one another over the festive period. You can even bring lover-boy with you." She winked and I blushed.

We walked slowly, arm in arm, eating cold toasted teacakes and not talking. The crisp air blew against my blushing cheeks, cool-ing them down as my embarrassment faded. I turned to watch my grandmother. She walked along the pavement as though it were a

catwalk, reminding me of Vanessa with every step she took. The half-smile etched across her face gave her an air of serenity that seemed out of place on the bustling and noisy Watling Avenue. For a moment I loved and idolised her more than anyone else in the world. I felt invincible and important in her presence and wanted to be with her forever. *I wish you were my mother.* The moment the thought entered my mind, I was shocked that I could display such a lack of loyalty.

"Whatever it is, don't feel so guilty about it. You haven't murdered anyone have you?"

"How can you tell, Grandma?"

"I'm not that different to you, darling, and I've been around a lot longer than you have."

"Have you ever thought things you shouldn't have?"

"Oh, plenty of times. I've done several things I shouldn't have too." She gave me her cheekiest grin and put my mind at ease.

The reception area of Edgware General was a bit of a shock to the system when one first entered. It was yellow-walled and grey-floored with a feeling of depressed resignation that seemed somehow trapped within its box. There was no flow there of any description. Even time seemed to stand still. The smell of stale smoke, wee and disinfectant permeated every crevice and the same beastly receptionist stared back at whoever approached the desk, day in, day out. I looked at the floor as she handed my grandmother a pen, her lifeless eyes betraying nothing. The glistening speckled floor mesmerised me for a while. I meant to watch my grandmother place her autograph in the signing-in book with the usual dramatic sweep that I loved so much, but I missed it, choosing instead to watch myself watch the floor. The curls on the back of my head caught the sunlight and glowed with an indigo hue… I felt peaceful and free, momentarily suspended in…

The back of my head… the back of my HEAD… the back of MY head?

Panic brought me back to my senses and I felt the horrible sick rushing sensation within the vessels of my head and ears again. I fell hard and fast, back into the paralysed form of Genevieve Kelly, the heart thumping life back into every cell, aching from the effort. Grandma looked at my sweaty face in horror, dragging me to the nearest loo before the vomit erupted from my startled mouth.

"Are you feeling ill, darling?"

My heart was beating in my throat. I couldn't answer so I shook my head.

"It's lucky we're in a hospital isn't it? I can take you back…"

"No. We've come this far. Curiosity will kill me before any bug does."

"That's my girl. You're a tough cookie, my darling. Not like your other flimsy relatives."

She grimaced with disgust as she wiped puke from my hair and flicked water on my face.

"Let's go and see what I have to show you."

Anna Cleary had been a friend of my grandmother's for several decades now. Her mother Claudia had been a jazz clarinettist and had met my grandmother in the West End during the Second World War. They often shared a taxi home in the early hours, for safety and also because my grandmother was terrified of dying alone in the Blitz.

"Oh, you should have seen us then. Claudia was a lot more outspoken than I was and, being a coloured girl, nobody wanted to associate with her on too deep a level. Things were different in those days, darling. If you were slightly out of the ordinary you were an outcast without exception."

"Nothing's changed then."

We both laughed.

Silence.

"Does it bother your mother that you're courting a coloured

boy, Genevieve? Please don't be offended. I think he's superb, up to a point."

"No. She just doesn't want me to have sex until I collect my pension. Has she said anything?"

"No."

"Even if she did, I don't care." I shrugged more than once, without meaning to. I felt a little uncomfortable. Joe's colour had never even registered in my psyche as a potential cause of friction. I made a mental note to watch my mother's body language more closely from now on. Grandma clasped her hands tightly over mine.

"Oh dear!" she wailed dramatically, "I can't remember the colour of Claudia's eyes!"

"Were they the same as Anna's?"

"No, Anna looks like her father. He was an American GI. Claudia never heard from him again and she couldn't trace him because they weren't legally married. She had no rights." She cocked her head and frowned. For a moment she reminded me of myself.

"Grandma?"

"It's age, dear."

"Oh." Grandma's grip eased and her face relaxed.

"Claudia died when Anna was only sixteen. I wanted to adopt her but she married that Larry chap. He treated her well, though." She laughed, suddenly looking very young. "There was nobody I could talk to when Kenneth passed away. The house was overrun with little boys. Anna and I became friends and have kept in touch ever since. I can't outlive her too, Genevieve."

"Does she have kids?"

"Yes, but children aren't always a guarantee that a person won't end up alone in the end." Something hit me in the centre of my breastbone, an invisible force. I felt a little twist in my heart, my grandmother's pain.

"Grandchildren could be though, right?" I asked, trying to lighten the mood.

"Yes, they can!"

She gave me a big, wet kiss on my forehead. I could sense the red, waxy splotch of lipstick on my skin, like a slimy imprint. The urge to wipe it off was strong but she was still looking at me so I had to exercise restraint. It was torturously difficult and I could feel a teenage 'hissy fit' coming on. I swallowed a few times but it didn't help. The lipstick felt alien on my skin and I could sense it crawling on the surface of me. Underneath it, I recoiled in horror.

Skin is a semi-permeable membrane. The lipstick cannot get through, Genevieve. Relax.

"Sorry, my darling."

Grandma pulled a handkerchief from her purse and wiped my forehead clean, but not before she had moistened it with her own spit. I could not take it anymore. Manners aside, I pulled my sleeve over my palm and wiped my head repeatedly for a good five minutes while she arranged the flowers in a jar by Anna's bed.

I'll have to bloody disinfect my head when I get home now! Aaargh!

Anna was wheeled into the ward in a trolley, propped up by huge billowing pillows. Her shiny bald head seemed to be engulfed by them and her tiny frightened eyes were sunken into her skull. She was so pale and fragile, like a bone china teacup, with skinny little fingers that gripped the edge of the sheet that covered her, as though for dear life. Still, she managed to smile warmly as my grandmother bent over and kissed her head. Her lipstick made a red smudge on Anna's shiny crown too.

I burst out laughing. There followed an uncomfortable silence as they both looked at me, confused.

"The red... the... it looks like a wax seal?" I said, as I twiddled my finger over my own crown, hinting. Neither of them understood what I was talking about so they started chatting between themselves about somebody called Elsie. I would have eaves-dropped but… *Wow. This is odd. But interesting. I wonder what it is.*

I became engrossed in what I saw, aware that I was staring but didn't care. Anna's bubble was full of holes like Marcus' old jeans when he had stubbed his cigarettes out on them. There was a slimy grey blob about the size of a football in the crook of her right arm, resting there. It looked like discoloured snot and smelled mildly putrid. It began to travel up her arm, spreading all over her body like a wave of greasy water. As it did so it burned new holes in her bubble, singeing it with its intensity.

I stepped back in fright, knocking against the opposite bed and bumping my thigh really hard. The knock hurt and confirmed the sad truth that this was no dream. Grandma and Anna looked at me momentarily and continued talking.

"Your grandchild's a bit clumsy, sweetie…."

How can you not feel that? You're covered in crap, it's seeping into your bones and you're having a laugh with my grandmother? I need air.

I walked outside and took a long, deep breath, the first I had taken for about an hour. I relaxed a little.

"Ouch, that's going to bruise!" I said aloud, as I noticed the painful tingling sensation in my thigh. "What the hell was that?" I said, even louder, hoping that the answer would come out of nowhere if I said it loudly enough.

"Chemotherapy."

I turned swiftly. It had come from my grandmother then.

"But why, Grandma?"

"Promise me you'll never forget what you saw, Genevieve."

"I won't, believe me. Why?"

"It's such a powerful treatment, darling, not everybody survives it. For some, it does more damage than good. I wanted you to see that."

"I don't understand."

"You will one day. Now let's go home for lunch. Bert's given me some tomatoes from his allotment."

But Anna had frightened me. I didn't know how deeply she had affected me until I realised a few weeks later that she was still in my thoughts, in front of me everywhere I looked. I spent every night that winter trying to escape the image of her chemotherapy.

Words could not describe how irritated I was by my parents. I was also annoyed with myself for allowing them to talk me out of my martial arts class so that they could take me to see Father Reilly.

"Genevieve, just speak to the Father," said my mother, as softly as she could, which by normal standards was not soft at all. "You'll feel so much better."

"I felt fine until now," I snapped.

"Just go along with it, Tiger. For my sanity as well as your own," begged Dad from the driver's seat.

I adjusted my seat belt and sat so that I was facing the window. The endless row of houses passed by at an even speed like a military tattoo. I noticed how many of the front gardens had been paved over for second and third family cars. It had dulled the energy of the thresholds without exception.

"You will both thank me for this one day," hissed Mum, as she plopped her handbag onto her lap and clasped her hands over it. Her knuckles were white.

"I don't even want to go!" I wailed at her, feeling a flood of hormones entering my brain and taking over my emotions. She ignored me.

"How can you think for one minute that a priest will transform me into some angel in one sitting?" I asked Dad. "I'm likely to turn *him* cuckoo. Whose side are you on anyway?"

Dad ignored me too. I watched as he flicked the indicator and turned the steering wheel deftly. He was a much better driver than my erratic mother and hardly ever suffered road rage. He was annoyingly slow though, especially when his children were passengers. Mum, on the other hand, swore like a navvy every time another car came near ours. She sometimes cursed in French when Dad was driving too and then tried to convince him that every word had been clean. I suddenly felt irritated again and decided to pass on the feeling.

"So, is he going to exorcise my demons then?" Neither of them acknowledged me. *Maybe a bit of stubbornness will help piss them off.* "I'm not going in, then."

"Tiger, you will go and speak to the bloody priest or Joe is banned from the goddamned house!" Mum and I both sucked in our breath for different reasons. She turned her head slowly towards Dad. *Uh oh.* Inside my head, I chuckled.

"Padraig? Blasphemy, the priest and our home in the same sentence?"

"Have I been struck by lightning, Eloise? No. So shut up both of you and let me drive in peace."

Further down the road Dad swerved to avoid a cat, hitting the curb and knocking off a hubcap.

"Aha!" Mum said, shuffling in her seat and looking triumphant. Nobody spoke for the rest of the journey.

Father Reilly was a good-looking man in his mid-thirties with a strong southern Irish accent. He rose from his seat as we walked through the back door of the church, into a small office with a kitchenette in the far corner. When I approached, he held out his hand and looked into my eyes as we shook hands. I warmed to him immediately.

"Do you mind if I speak to Genevieve alone? I can leave the door open if it makes you feel more comfortable."

"No, no, we'll go and pray for a while," said Mum. "Genevieve can come and get us when she's ready to leave."

I watched my parents leave the room. Dad turned and gave me

a thumbs-up signal before Mum pulled him out and shut the door.
I heard muffled chiding outside that died down very quickly.

"Would you like some tea, Genevieve?"

"No thanks, I don't drink tea."

"Why is that then?"

"Milk gives me gas."

"Can I offer you some herbal tea?" I had never tried herbal tea.
In fact, I had never heard of it before.

"Okay. What's herbal tea?"

"Tea made from other types of plants or fruit peel or spices."

"Sounds yum, I think."

I looked around me with great respect. Father Reilly's of-
fice/kitchen was full of jars of different shapes and sizes, filled
with leaves and powders and dried roots. I smiled at him as he
handed me a mug of delicious-smelling lemon and ginger tea.
Unfortunately, it smelled a lot better than it tasted.

*What a bloody let-down. Oops, I said bloody in church. Bloody
hell, not again. Well, I've bloody well done it now. Why is it when you
try to avoid thinking about something, you bloody well think of it
more?*

"Your parents are worried about you, you know."

"I know."

"Do you know why?"

"Mum thinks I'm insane."

"No, she doesn't. She just thinks you need a bit of direction.
You have to admit, you've given her some cause for concern."

"And you're going to give me that direction?"

"No, I'm just here to listen if you need someone to talk to other than your parents. And it's all strictly confidential. I promise."

I have Matthew for that.

I studied Father Reilly's hands. They were practical hands like
Mum's, only bigger and with slight discoloration on the pads of
the fingertips. The fingernails had dirt embedded in them, so

deep that it would have been impossible to get it all out even with a needle.

"You're a gardener?" I asked.

"Yes, you're very observant. What gave me away?"

"The dirt on your hands. The rest of you is clean so it's not because you don't wash properly. Must be mud, then."

"Do you grow things, Genevieve?"

"No."

"What do you do in your spare time?"

"To keep me sane, you mean?"

He laughed.

"I go for Tae Kwon Do lessons. I draw and write. I walk a lot. I love being outside. Trees and animals interest me a lot. What do you grow?"

"Herbs, mainly. They're great for treating maladies. If you have the time and the inclination, I can teach you. It's a very ancient science that all cultures share."

"Botany?"

"Naturopathy and herbalism."

Father Reilly intrigued me. He was not the stuffy, religious zealot I had imagined him to be. He did not perform any exorcisms or preach verses from the Bible. In fact, we spent the next hour discussing Joe, school and the benefits of vegetarianism. When the conversation wound down naturally, I went outside to search for my parents. They were sitting in the front row of the church in silence, hand in hand. Seeing them so close, I realised how important bringing me here was to them, and decided that it wouldn't hurt to see Father Reilly on occasion, if only to learn about herbalism. That way I would be expanding my knowledge and Mum would feel some relief that I was taking an interest in church. I still didn't fully understand how organised religion could be so important to her. In my view, it made her rigid and short-sighted but if it gave me some respite and her less to worry about then I was willing to give it a chance. They smiled at me as I approached and Mum got up and tidied my hair, a gesture that was the equivalent of a hug from her. I wandered outside as they said their goodbyes to Father Reilly and ended up in the graveyard.

"You can see me?" asked a voice without a body.

"No."

"Turn around."

I turned to find myself in front of a simple grave, long since faded by the ravages of time and weather. On the headstone sat a young man of about thirty with peppermint-green eyes and a thick mane of hair. He wore a dirty shirt and brown trousers and looked like a labourer.

"You can see me!"

"Yes. Why?"

"Somebody can see me and hear me. Somebody to speak to! Hurrah!"

"Are you Scottish?"

"Yes. My accent, isn't it?"

"Yes, I can tell. Why are you so relieved to see me?"

"I don't know what to do. I can't find my wife anywhere. In fact, I can't find anyone or recognise anything."

"Do you know that you're dead?"

"I'm what?"

"You're dead. Is that your grave?"

"No. I'm not sure. How do you know I'm dead?"

"By the fact that nobody else can see you, you're wearing out of date clothes and you can't see anyone else even though there are lots of people living around here."

"I feel lighter suddenly. Maybe that's what I needed to know. Many thanks, young lady."

He vanished and the atmosphere cleared. I looked up at the blue sky streaked with cirrus clouds and began to understand the principle of randomness.

Nothing is really random, is it? Everything happens for a reason. I wonder what I'm here for.

For a fleeting moment, I felt at one with everything, as though I was exactly where I was meant to be at that particular second in time. The moment quickly passed and I became confused and frustrated Genevieve Kelly once more, a square peg in a round hole.

"Genevieve! Genevieve! Qu'est ce que tu fais?"

"Nothing. Coming Mum," I grumbled, and made my way back to the car.

Grandma took me to watch an orchestral recital on the South Bank for my seventeenth birthday. We both had a real passion for classical music, one that I kept hidden from everyone except her. It was our little secret.

"Had I been two hundred years older, darling, I think I would have had a terrible crush on Mozart," she told me as we listened to his Requiem with our eyes closed.

"Wasn't he a little mad, Grandma?"

"Aren't we all?" she answered, without opening her eyes. We had travelled to the South Bank by Tube. It had taken me hours to coax her into taking the Underground. She was snobbish about certain forms of public transport and thought all Underground trains dirty and full of people with terrible body odour.

"Darling, how can you *want* to take an Underground train? You're armpit height!"

"It's really not that bad. And it's part of the experience. We can walk along the river before the concert."

"Ugh! An hour on the sooty, smelly, disgusting London Underground system… Ugh! Please don't do that to me!"

"Think of the stroll - the London by moonlight that you love so much, the well-dressed people walking along the Thames, many going to the same concert." That had swayed her. She loved walking and the London skyline. This way she could experience the best of both and it was worth an hour on the Tube. I watched as her face softened, the stubbornness giving way to a semi-smile. She turned to me, chin raised. Her head was cocked slightly to the right, which meant she was going to be authoritative. The left meant she was about to be affectionate.

"Oh, alright, but just remember you're as stubborn as I am and it doesn't get better with age."

"I can deal with that, Grandma."

As we walked arm in arm towards the South Bank I had the feeling that something huge was about to happen. I often got a stirring sensation in my gut just before a major event or situation but this was different; the sensation was in my heart and it felt as though something was desperately trying to break free. I felt annoyed with it; this was my time with my grandmother and yet I was not able to give her the attention I wanted to because of the incessant squirming in my chest. After a while I rubbed my chest but that only made it worse. It was as though touch had given it a life of its own.

We had decent seats in the concert hall, two-thirds of the way up and near the door so that my grandmother could run to the bathroom as soon as we were allowed to leave in the interval. She was under the impression that she was becoming incontinent because all women of her age were supposed to be, although I was sure that this was purely her imagination. As I looked around the hall, I felt the energy and passion of all the performances that had taken place before. The acoustics were wonderful, every little noise and splutter was grabbed from the air and thrown back down without repeating itself. It made the place seem cavernous and vast, perfect for the delicate sounds of the instruments.

As the music started, something began to happen to the musicians. Huge vortices opened up beneath their chairs and from their throats. Their bubbles became huge and columns of colour sprouted from their tiny heads. As they continued to play, their bubbles merged and filled the room but did not suffocate. Some of the streams of light that moved around the concert hall touched me, melting into my body and producing a rush of energy that travelled up my spine and produced tears of pleasure in my eyes. The energy was unlike anything I had physically experienced before. I breathed it in and looked down as the creature in my heart began to bang against my breast-bone furiously. It eventually broke free as a beautiful pink stream of love, releasing me into the room and suspending me in the air high above, where I could feel it all happening around me. I watched as the arcs of beautiful colour stretched around the room, bridging gulfs between everything that existed there.

Music looks like Heaven!

The evening of the recital was the defining moment in my life. We all have moments, one single space in time that is ours. For that small aeon of time I felt as though I were home. It was the only time I truly belonged.

ELEVEN

Reaching Out

I'm on loan to this Earth.
I don't know what for but I've got to
make good whatever time I have.

As part of his benefits package, Marcus' employers had given him a mobile telephone called a Mercury One-to-One. It was a daft-looking contraption that resembled something between a brick and a slug. Personally I didn't see the point of it but Joe was seduced. He gasped in wonder when the keys glowed as Marcus started dialling.

"Wow Gen, look at that!"

"Call her Gene," teased Marcus.

"Not if you want to live," I retorted.

"It even stores important numbers and works pretty much everywhere over ground." Joe gawped.

"I wish I had that effect on you," I said, unable to keep the sarcasm out of my voice. I folded my arms and waited.

"I need it for work," said Marcus proudly.

"What, so you can wank - I mean bank - on the go?" I asked. By this time I was visibly irritated.

"Tsk, Genevieve!" Mum stood behind us with a dishcloth in her hands. *Great timing.* She was too busy throwing the dishcloth at me to notice Marcus put four fingers up at me, two on each hand. *As usual, great timing Marcus.*

Suddenly, I heard Vanessa's voice loud and clear in my head. She needed money. The smell of smoke filled my nostrils, my hands felt so cold they ached and I was hungry, very hungry. I was craving something without knowing what it was. All I knew was that I had to have it.

Marcus's `phone rang.

It's Vanessa. She's feeding an addiction. I can feel it. It's horrible. My stomach hurts but food will make me fat and ugly. Need something. These are not my feelings.

Joe grabbed me.

"Gen, you've gone blue."

"Mon dieu! Genevieve!" Mum was panicking.

I began to cry.

"I'm so hungry. My tummy hurts."

I didn't know how else to articulate what I felt so I looked at my mother helplessly in the hope that maternal instinct would save the day. She ran to the kitchen. I could hear the fridge door slam and several pots and pans clanking. Meanwhile Marcus' tone of voice was getting angrier and angrier. He had taken the call out in the hallway for privacy but I could hear him loud and clear.

"...I can't come over to bloody Paris... I'm not going to... you earn shit loads yourself... what? How can you be broke?"

I listened carefully.

"Fine, Saturday at seven, Embankment. Don't waste my time!"

That was all I needed to know.

"Why are you smiling Gen?" asked Joe. He was searching my face with his eyes.

"Because you're holding my hands."

"Just warming them up for you before your mum gets back."

If Joe's face had been any closer to mine I would have kissed him then. Instead I blushed and looked away. Through the crack in the door I detected somebody watching us. Evelyn pushed the door open slowly and stood directly in front of us, glaring mercilessly.

"What a draught! Here, don't let your hands get any colder," Joe said as he covered them with a scatter cushion.

Evelyn's face cracked a little to make way for a hideously sadistic smile.

"Behaving like a little whore? I'll teach you." Her voice was deep and menacing. Still, I showed no fear, only raising an eyebrow at her. Mum swept in and unwittingly dispersed Evelyn so that her molecules disappeared into the ether. *Not if I teach you first, you old bat. You abused John Graham and I'll never let you forget it.*

With a clattering of plates, Mum served up three portions of toasted cheese and tomato sandwiches and yelled for Marcus to come and sit down. I continued to watch the doorway until Mum took my chin and turned my face towards her. She looked into my eyes, searching. *You'll never find it, Mum, whatever it is you are looking for.*

That Saturday Joe was away at a football match with the school team. The coach had treated them to a real game, hoping it would convince at least one of them to play professionally instead of going to university. It was the perfect opportunity to follow Marcus and Joe had offered to cover for me. He trusted me implicitly and asked no questions as to where I was going and what I was going for. I told him, for my sake as well as his, because sooner or later I would have burst. After Vanessa had left, Mum had told everybody we knew that she'd been offered a contract in Milan. In reality we had no idea where she was; until now, that is.

It was obvious that Marcus was not going on a date that Saturday night. He made no effort to shave or co-ordinate his clothing and didn't bother with hair gel. I also decided to become as non-descript as possible, opting for faded jeans and an old hooded jacket that I'd picked up at a charity shop that afternoon. I'd also purchased a New York Yankees baseball cap and empty glasses frames at the same shop. Joe and I pretended to leave and walked to the corner shop where he bade me goodbye. I waited until Marcus walked by and put on the unfamiliar attire before following him to Edgware Station.

The board outside the station warned of delays and, after a few words with the station attendant, Marcus turned and walked out to the shopping centre. I dived behind the florist's stall just as he passed by and scrambled to my feet as he blended into the crowds of Saturday shoppers.

"Genevieve! Oi!"

Bugger crap shit! Who the hell could that be? How the hell did he recognise me? What?

Ravi caught up with me and started to talk about something. I had no idea what it was because I was trying to keep Marcus in sight. He disappeared from view near W H Smith.

Shit!

"Well, will you let your parents know?"

"Know? Eh?"

People, particularly women, were moving more slowly around us, some even stopping to appreciate Ravi. It made finding Marcus more difficult and I was beginning to panic.

"Genevieve, have you not been listening to a word I've been saying?"

"Er, no, sorry. What is it?" He rolled his eyes in disbelief, in much the same way as Joe did. It was bizarre to see.

"I'm having a party to celebrate my twenty-first. One for the olds. There's another one but you're too young for that."

"Yeah, okay, we'll come. Can I go now?"

"You're weird, Genevieve. But you're yourself. I like that."

I had spotted Marcus' jacket milling through the people heading towards the exit nearest the station. By the time I passed the bus depot it had vanished. I made my way to the station attendant near the ticket barriers.

"I'm looking for my brother. He's about six two with auburn hair and a cruddy brown leather jacket?"

"Just went through. Your brother is he?"

The station attendant looked me up and down a few times. I now understood why Vanessa often displayed the bad attitude she did. Being as attractive as she was must have been difficult to cope with as she was growing up. I took my cue from her.

"Why are you looking at me like that? Just let me through."

I ran as fast as I could, only to see the train slowly slide away from the platform, picking up speed by the second. In the last carriage, Marcus had opened up a newspaper, dropping the junk mail inside it onto his lap. I skulked back to the station attendant.

"Without looking me up and down, can you tell me when the next train is due?"

"Thirty minutes."

"What?"

"Engineering works."

I hope you fall arse-first in your birthday cake, Ravi.

It was getting dark outside by the time I left the station, shoulders drooping but fingers tightly curled into a fist. I took several deep breaths before I calmed down enough to remember that Joe and I were supposed to be out together and that I had nowhere to go. That night I taught myself how to climb trees without breaking any twigs. I felt drawn to the old church by the crossroads and jumped over the stone wall into the graveyard that seemed somehow welcoming. Like an ape I jumped from tree to tree in the churchyard off Station Road, careful not to fall onto the gravestones below. Nobody saw me and I told nobody. For the next two hours I was totally free, encased and protected by the darkness, able to shed tears that needed to be shed that night. It was my odd little secret and took my mind off Vanessa for a brief while. Deep down inside I missed her terribly but refused to admit it to anyone, including myself. The only thing my pride would allow me to admit to would be the curiosity I felt whenever I thought about her. Years later, when I realised that we were not to meet again before my death, I would wonder why I didn't make more of an effort to follow Marcus that evening.

Next day, I went to church of my own accord. To avoid my parents and grandmother, I chose to go to Whitchurch after lunch when there would be nobody there other than myself and God. I was prepared to feel like a traitor to the Catholic Church but I didn't, because Whitchurch was the same as our usual Sunday morning Catholic haunt, albeit with a different name. Ever since we had moved I had wanted to visit Whitchurch and take a look at the place that had played such a huge part in Matthew's short life. I wasn't sure what I expected to find, maybe a hint or an imprint of Matthew that had remained there for over two centuries. It proved to be a high expectation that inevitably led to disappointment. So many people had passed through the doors of Whitchurch since then that the air was a melee of voices and energies, so tightly strung together it was impossible to part them. I took a seat in the pew furthest away from the front and waited with my eyes closed.

Nothing.

Maybe it's because I don't know what I'm praying for. In fact, I'm not even praying. I should go home but I like it here. It's quiet.

Eventually I decided to leave. My lack of purpose was making me increasingly self-conscious and I worried about being asked to go because I looked shifty. It was a beautiful day outside and I began to walk in the direction of my gut feeling. If a place or road looked inviting, I would walk towards it or along it. I had no idea where I would end up, but playing the game excited me more than the destination. Edgware was a small suburb and I thought I'd seen it all, but that day I discovered streets I'd never heard of, places I had no idea existed and people I had never greeted before. Almost two hours later I began to feel the ache in my feet and calves. It was time to stop, except there was nowhere I could sit down comfortably for longer than a minute.

What would I do even if I could sit down? There's nobody here to watch go by. I wish Joe were here.

"Argh! And I still don't know what 'arse in a jar' means! Why won't somebody tell me?" I yelled at nothing in particular. A cough startled me and I jumped up, swallowing my heart back down as I tried to bring the beating under control. I was rarely startled.

"It's just me, Genevieve," said an embarrassed Father Reilly. He was in civvy garb today and carrying about six bags of shopping.

"Can I help you with those?" I offered.

"Okay, but only if you stay for a cup of tea."

"Okay."

Father Reilly's library was a fascinating place. He must have had every book on botany ever written. The bookcases were stacked so high that he kept a stepladder handy in case he couldn't reach the one he was after. I was also impressed by his memory, as he knew the exact location of each book and what its contents were. He left me there to browse while he went to tend to his garden. I sauntered towards the row of jars on his windowsill. They had no labels on them so I opened each one up to smell its contents.

"Hmm, rosemary."

Wonder what this one is. Gross! It smells like a bog!

My stomach lurched so I decided to give up being nosey and looked for a book that I could read instead. I looked around me and began to feel very uncomfortable. The feeling of leaden legs and queasiness came back gradually and I began to feel a strong urge to go home. But there was something keeping me back.

That book is so lovely and red. As I reached out for it, the shelf above gave way and at least a dozen books came crashing down on me, stunning me for a second. One had fallen into my lap, wide open, inviting me to read its contents. It was very dusty. As I brushed off the waste of years of neglect, the last word on the page caught my eye.

Arse-

I held my breath and stared at it, paralysed.

Arse in a jar, arse in a jar, arse in a jar. What could it be?

The open window let in a gust of breeze that lifted the page and pushed it over.

The words didn't mean anything for a split second.

... arsenicum. Often used in the late 17th and 18th centuries to whiten a noble lady's complexion, arsenic (commonly known as) was later discovered to be a poison and a carcinogen...

Matthew's words rang in my ears.

... often called 'the poison of kings' it was popular due to the fact that it was colourless and odourless and could be mixed into food or drink... symptoms were not immediate, depending on dosage, and included fever, sweats, abdominal cramps, hair loss, vomiting and excruciating pain towards the end...

The breath I had unconsciously held suddenly escaped and I came back to my senses.

"The bitch murdered them. Oh shit, I didn't mean to swear in church."

I was still sitting on the floor, hugging the book, when Father Reilly returned. He must have thought I had suffered a head injury because I remember a doctor shining a light into my eyes and my Dad carrying me to the car.

That night and the night after, I did not sleep. Rage and anxiety pushed enough blood to my brain to prevent any rest, however brief. The realisation that Margaret and Michael had been poisoned spun around and around my head with no sign of stopping. There would be no respite for me. I knew Evelyn had been nasty and abusive, but being a murderess added a whole new dimension to her character and the enmity between us. I loved the Davises like a second family now and I knew that they needed justice. However, I also knew that I was not beyond Evelyn's grasp and had to tread very carefully now.

Well, Genevieve, if anyone can think of a fool-proof plan and wait for the right moment to execute it, it's you. There's got to be a way…

The stars twinkled at me, returning my smile. As I sat on the roof feeling their gaze upon my face, I thought about them and what they had done for me over the years. They had listened, comforted and shown me affection and I considered them a long-lost family. The first night I had discovered the roof was a Saturday and as usual Mum and Vanessa had been yelling at one another. Vanessa had wanted to go to a party and Mum had refused to allow it. I could still hear them arguing inside my head.

"I want to go!"

"No, Vanessa!"

"Why?"

"They're older than you!"

"Exactly!"

"What? Why 'exactly' Vanessa? What do you mean?"

"It means I'm cool enough to be invited, even though I'm younger than them!"

"And what if they drink? What if some older boy takes advantage of you? Then what?"

"Listen to yourself! Nobody is going to take advantage!"

"I asked 'then what' so answer me!"

The noise had made me feel physically ill but, being so young, I only had two options, to hide or escape. I chose to head straight for the exit that would take me in the opposite direction to the noise – the window of my bedroom. There was a decent-sized windowsill outside and a sloping roof. I had dislodged a roof tile, sending it slithering and then crashing down on to the paving below.

My heart had stopped for a second. But the arguing continued so I made myself comfortable on the windowsill, curling up tightly until I could rest my chin on my knees.

A whole new world opened up for me that night. The peacefulness and clarity of the dotted indigo sky made time stand still for me then. It held me in its protective embrace and I wept, knowing that home was so close that I could feel it and yet would never be within my mortal reach. Since then, I had regularly visited the stars. They were my confidants, my true friends, my community.

Now I sat with face turned towards them, eyes closed. I had nothing to offer them other than my smile. My heart bled to be with them, to go back to where I belonged and so desperately missed, but I knew that time was not now. I opened my eyes as they bade me to, not looking down for a moment.

I'm on loan to this Earth. I don't know what for but I've got to make good whatever time I have.

My smile grew. Soon I would begin a new phase in my life, the next stage of the journey was nigh. The stars would be the only friends to come with me.

Marcus was visibly annoyed at the dinner table. His annoyance kept poking me in the stomach and putting me off my food. Yet another girlfriend had dumped him after spending a large portion of the month's salary. Mum and Dad had felt the need to 'have a chat' with him about his personal life, first turning his heartbreak into anger and then giving it fuel and moulding it into simmering resentment.

He's going to grow a paunch if he's not careful. I watched the gloopy emotion resting on his abdomen. *It reminds me of a gargoyle.*

My parent's chat was supposed to be a gentle talk with Marcus, to gauge what he was looking for and why he kept repeating the same mistake over and over again.

"Marcus, you change girlfriends like underwear. Why?" asked Mum, being her usual diplomatic self.

"Thanks a lot!" shouted Marcus, as loud as he could but to little effect.

"It's becoming ridiculous, son. With the amount you earn, you should be investing in property or something," said Dad. Marcus folded his arms, creating a physical barrier between himself and them. His bubble solidified. Dad didn't move.

"What I do with my income is none of your business." Marcus' voice was so low and menacing that I walked out of the room. Upstairs I changed into my pyjamas and climbed out of the window.

I wonder why women dump him after spending his money. He might be my brother but even I can admit he's very handsome and clever. Doesn't that make him a catch? Maybe he's really boring. After what seemed like an eternity I heard the front door slam and Dad was telling Mum off.

"Eloise, we're going for a drive. No buts! You'll drive him away saying things like that!"

"He's stupid!" wailed Mum, in a very French accent.

"We're driving, so calm down!"

The car doors slammed and the engine started. Below me Marcus had lit a cigarette. I watched the glowing orange spot bob up and down in the darkness as Marcus walked to the apple tree and sat down next to it. He took out his mobile and dialled a number. I shifted in discomfort as the keypad illuminated his profile, turning him into an eerie apparition.

"I just got a bollocking from the parents and it's all your fault, you parasite!" he yelled. A shower of spit glowed green for a second as it left his mouth. I held my breath and retreated further back into the darkness of the window frame. "They think it's my girlfriends spending my bank balance when the reality is that I can't afford girlfriends because of you!" He was shouting at Vanessa. I still held my breath. "Just piss off out of my life, Vanessa. I've had enough."

Marcus' pain hit me in the stomach and I began to retch. Worried that he might detect my presence, I took a deep breath and held it again. Eventually he stubbed out his cigarette and went back inside, slamming the back door behind him really hard. The resulting shockwave rippled through the air and along the walls, dissipating the rage a little. I climbed back into my room and breathed again. *Ah, that feels much better.*

"Genevieve!" roared Marcus from downstairs. I felt the door shudder as he stamped up the stairs. He may have been enraged but I was not afraid of him the way I was of Mum or Vanessa. "It's so bloody cold in here! Have you left the bloody window open again?" he bellowed from just outside my door. I could see his shadow through the crack underneath. Still, I didn't consider him to be a monster or a threat of any kind. "I'm talking to you!" He was not going to go away.

Think fast!

"Don't come in, I'm naked," was all I could think of.

"What? In that freezing room? Rubbish!" He yanked the door open and stood there, eyes narrowed.

"Joe's been here hasn't he?"

"Eh?"

"I'll bet he's just climbed out of the window!" Marcus opened the window and stuck his head out. Unlike me, he did not have to climb on to the sill to do that. He turned around and glared at me. "You'd better watch it. As it is, everyone thinks you're mentally ill. At this rate, you'll get a reputation too."

"From what I heard, Marcus, it's not me with the reputation."

"You little freak!"

Marcus punched me in the face, not hard enough to knock me over but enough to stun both of us. I could see the look of shock on his face. Suddenly, he grew angry again.

"You know why Vanessa left? Because of you! You freaked her out, embarrassed her every single day. It's all your fault, you irritant! You should've gone instead!"

I'd heard enough. I punched Marcus in the groin as hard as I could. It was more to shut him up than out of anger or nastiness. I was more hurt than anything else and, as the tears flowed, I ran out of the door barefoot, all the way to Joe's house.

I almost lost a toenail climbing up the drainpipe that ran alongside Joe's bedroom window. Luckily he was in his room, propped up on the floor, cleaning his football boots. He scowled as he held them up to the light before putting them down on newspaper he had laid out especially. I decided to watch him a little longer and withdrew the hand I had extended to knock with.

Joe was too big for his box room. He was so long that his dad had built him an extra-long bed the moment his feet had started to poke out of the other end. I still remembered the day his dad had presented it to him. He had asked me to take Joe to the Trocadero for at least six hours (he was very precise) so that he could fix the frame high up on the wall, giving Joe the entire floor space for his belongings. It had been a superb idea at the time but Joe grew and grew until it was virtually impossible for him to sleep straight. Sometimes he would resort to sleeping diagonally across the floor on a sleeping bag his parents had had since their student days. I suggested he swap rooms with Ravi, Ravi being at least four inches shorter and owning little except hair gel and clothes.

Joe's dad would not hear of it though, explaining that Ravi needed the extra space to study. It made little sense to me but there was nothing I could do to change his mind.

Joe yawned and stretched, bumping his elbow on the wall. My chest fluttered a little and then went still.

One day I'll make sure you have a huge room to sleep in with a large bed and a beautiful cabinet for your trophies. I love you more than anything and anybody.

Joe turned around and fell backwards in fright when he saw me.

"For heaven's sake, Genevieve!" he said, opening the window and gently lifting me in. "You look like a ghost in the darkness out there." He paused for a second, looking me up and down. "How long have you been out there? It's freezing and you're not wearing much. What happened to your toe? Hold on, why aren't you in shoes? And what the hell happened to your face? Who hit you?"

"Marcus and I had a fight. He punched me so I punched him back and ran."

"Marcus punched you? I'll kill him!"

"Wait! Joe!"

Joe had grabbed his coat and was trying to put his shoes on. I snatched one of them and sat on it.

"Give me the shoe, Gen."

"No."

"I'll start shouting and my parents will…"

"They're not even here, Joe."

He hesitated and his posture relaxed. I knew what he was thinking.

"Their car isn't in the drive and the front lights aren't on. Yours is the only inhabited room in the back other than Ravi's and he's at university. You no longer leave lights on unnecessarily because I keep nagging you about the ozone layer."

Joe sat on the floor, defeated.

"You're too clever for me, you know that?"

"No, I don't know that. Let's watch a movie on TV or something. Hey, the X-Files is on now, right?"

As I curled up next to him on the sofa, I smiled. He had been ready to fight Marcus for me. *To defend my honour. I wonder who'd have won? They're evenly matched in height. Marcus is smarter but Joe's got a bad temper. Well, if Marcus had started to win I'd have joined in to help Joe. We'll be spending evenings like this on the sofa when we're married.*

I noticed Joe's hands moving under my clothing, making me tingle with pleasure. It was not that I didn't want to go any further but we were only just seventeen. Besides, I was Catholic and terrified of the consequences. Suddenly, he threw me aside and got up.

"I think you'd better go, Gen." His gaze was resting on my boobs for once. I too looked down at the virtually flat terrain of my chest, wondering how it could possibly tempt him. The `phone rang and Joe went to answer it.

"That was your dad. Look, Gen, I'll walk you home, okay?"

"Okay."

"We'll have to talk about this later, alright? I'm sorry, I didn't mean to scare you."

"It's okay, Joe, really."

I had braced myself for an argument when I got home but instead Mum had welcomed us both with open arms. She was horrified when she saw the bruising on my face and realised I must have been terribly frightened or upset to have run away barefoot and in my pyjamas. Joe became the gallant hero who had rescued me and brought me home, putting him firmly in Mum's good books for the next ten years, even though he wasn't Catholic.

Joe and I never did have that conversation about sex. Ten months later I was gone but not forgotten, and our relationship became a romantic one across sea and time, giving it room to grow and blossom.

TWELVE

Leaving

Seventeen years on Earth and this is all I have?

At times the frustration I felt with life was so strong that it threatened to consume me, turning me into a clandestine monster. I could not explode. The very nature of explosion was messy and went against my character. What was I to do? It took every ounce of self-control not to allow it to unleash a savage beast that could never be reined in again. How I wished I could have talked openly to my mother, to share my thoughts with her and form the basis for some kind of relationship. But there was no point; she would never have acknowledged it. She had spent the last seventeen years wasting her time, intelligence and energy not knowing who I was. Instead, she had constructed her own version of Genevieve, a mythical concept of what she thought I ought to be. Sometimes I hated her for it and I harboured a deep mistrust of her for years.

Just before my first A Level exam, I cracked. The day had been no different to any other. We didn't argue, or 'have a discussion' as she liked to call it. She was stomping from one radiator to another, collecting dry laundry and flinging it into the basket that was bouncing off her hip. When there was no more laundry to collect, she slammed the basket onto my essay folder, the resultant draught turning several pages of the book I was taking notes from.

"Genevieve, why do you not brush your hair properly? It's everywhere."

"I'm studying. I don't need tidy hair to study." I did not attempt to hide the irritation in my voice because she didn't understand subtlety. She remained where she stood, looking at me, annoying me further.

"What are you studying, Genevieve?"

"The Wife of Bath's Tale. Here, why don't you take a look?" I opened the book, seemingly at random, but knowing very well that it was at a rather explicit point in the story. *That'll show you. You've never listened to me anyway. Why should I care?* I watched as her lips pursed up and she put the book down. She did not look pretty like that, just older.

"Qu'est-ce que c'est?"

"Medieval porn, but beautifully written."

"You are…"

"What? Mad? Turning into Vanessa? Rude? What?" My voice was irritatingly lazy as I couldn't be bothered to shout. She began to narrow her eyes and then widen them again. I had observed her long enough to guess what she meant by that. *Here comes the damn guilt trip.* I rolled my eyes and folded my arms to protect my stomach against a potentially appetite-destroying argument. *I'm not going to entertain this for a second.*

"How could you hurt me like this, Genevieve?"

"It's called Chaucer. We study it at school because it's literature, not because we know it'll shock you. Get over yourself."

"Imbecile!" she cried.

How the hell do I shut her up? Out of sheer frustration, I exposed myself.

"Marguerite's about to call you. She's going to invite you to a barbeque to celebrate her son's engagement. She's wearing jeans and an old lilac jumper she found in the attic after twenty years. She had her hair cut an hour ago and has just put some cakes in the oven. Her little finger's bandaged." Mum stared at me. It had worked. The 'phone began to ring.

"Aren't you going to pick it up?" I asked, betraying irritation in my voice again. *For God's sake, I wanted to shut you up, not stupefy you further.* Dad picked up the cordless upstairs and walked down with it. His heavy footsteps resounded through the house and cut through the shock and silence in the dining room.

"Of course we'd love to come," I heard him say, "and save some of those for me. You know I have to maintain my figure." He patted his paunch. Mum snatched the 'phone as he opened his mouth to speak again.

"Marguerite, what are you wearing? ... Aha, and where did you find it? ... Oh no, I'm just playing a game with Genevieve." Her tanned face became pale as the blood drained away. I maintained a calm façade but inside I was shaking. Would she accept me now? It didn't matter – I couldn't live like this anymore.

Whether she accepted me or not, I knew I'd done the right thing, even if it did bring her world tumbling down. Mum put the 'phone on the table when she was finished and turned to face me. I was shocked at the hatred in her eyes.

"Genevieve, get out of my house!"

"Hold on, Eloise, what's she done now?" asked Dad, as shocked as I was by her tone.

"She's the devil's child and I will not have her in my house anymore!"

"It's my house too, and I say she stays. You're being utterly unreasonable."

"She's mad!"

"And I can see where she gets it from!"

As my parents commenced arguing, it dawned on me that things were never going to change. I sighed and left the house, walking slowly in the sunshine to clear my head.

I sat at a table by the window, staring at the sun-drenched street outside. The library was quiet except for the whirring sound from a dormant photocopier in the corner. There were several other students in the room but I was the only one not studying. My mind was playing a game with me, registering traces of Evelyn Bingham in all the people I watched pass by.

My A Levels were an odd time of stasis for me. The process of acquiring knowledge was something I enjoyed, but having then to show how much of it I had actually absorbed was something I felt almost indifferent to. At school, there was a tinge of panic in the air mixed with expectation and dread which I could not tap into or share; however hard I tried, I just couldn't feel the same negative emotions that had taken over the lives of my peers. Exams were just another chapter in my life and a small door to my future through which I could peek occasionally with my imagination. At best, they were a mildly exciting challenge but most days were just routine.

Even Joe looked confused and frightened during this supposedly intense period. I had watched him over the last few weeks, staring into the distance as he nervously chewed the end of his pen. His fear had become localised to his stomach and so thick that it almost got between us when we hugged. Because of this fear we chose not to see one another more than once a week during exam time.

My thoughts shifted back to Evelyn. She had interrupted them on a daily basis since I had pieced together what she had done. Her presence was making me feel uncomfortable in my own home, not to mention annoyed. There was no longer any fear of her in my heart because now that I had grown up I was able to see her as she truly was - an old hag, twisted by her own bitterness. I wondered how things might have been for Evelyn had she chosen differently. Had there never been an opportunity for her to do so? Even so, she should have had the strength to make one; she was not a shrinking violet. There must have been a point in her life that had amounted to a crossroads, a do-or-die situation that stripped everything back to simple choices that could have opened up a wealth of new experience. Maybe she had just chosen to remain at the crossroads and her bitterness was merely the putrefying indecision that poisoned her from the inside?

Whatever the answers, Evelyn had to go. I did not want her in my home any more. She simply had to go.

"How do I get rid of her?" I whispered to myself.

Realising that I was not going to get any more work done, I put my books in my bag and left the library. It was a beautiful summer day and it drew me to the nearest green space where I sat in silence for a while.

"You asked a question," said a gruff voice.

"Sorry? Who are you?" I asked the rather unkempt man standing in front of me.

"Malcolm," he chortled, then added as an afterthought, "I'm the gardener here."

"Hello, Malcolm," I said as I smiled and lifted my face to the skies. The sun beat down on me and for a moment I was surrounded by an orange haze that cradled me outside my body, in a space just above my own head.

"How did you know I'd asked a question?"

"How do you know that John is real?"

I was pulled back into reality with a massive thud. As the perspiration popped up through my pores I took a better look at the man leaning on a spade in front of me. He had crystal blue eyes of a shade I had never seen before. They glowed within his skull and looked almost out of place in his human body.

"Point taken," I said and moved over so that he could share the bench. "Sorry, I didn't realise the rest of the bench was covered in bird doo-doo. I would have moved over sooner."

"That's okay, lady. That question you asked about an hour ago - just talk to her. She's a woman too."

"How… how did you…? Come back here! Please!" I called after him as he walked away. He didn't stop and nor did he look back, eventually disappearing into the hazy heat of the evening and leaving me with no choice but to seek out Evelyn.

Joe and I lay on the warm grass, toasting ourselves. We lay in our usual spot under the weeping willow tree in Canons Park, with me in the shade to avoid burning and he in the sun to promote a deeper tan. Joe enjoyed being in the sun. He had his eyes closed but was not asleep. The contented smile that loosened his face reflected peaceful relaxation. We were exactly where we wanted to be at that particular moment in time. The definition of bliss.

I turned towards him and rested my head on his chest, feeling his heart beat underneath. *All that separates us is the skin and bone in between.* Joe stirred but did not get up.

"Gen, promise me again that you'll come back and marry me. I'm going to start putting money away so we can get a house together. I'm not dreaming am I?" I laughed. He looked so sweet and innocent when he said that.

"I promise. Again. We're going to see each other regularly and we're definitely going to get married."

He closed his eyes again, happy. I put my left hand up to the light and allowed the tiny diamond to sparkle in the sunshine. Over the last two years, Joe had saved his odd-job wages in order to buy me a proper engagement ring. I gazed at it. Somehow it made my hand look perfect.

"Mrs Johann Bose," I declared loudly. Joe looked up, genuinely surprised.

"I've never heard you say my full name before."

"Really?"

"Yeah, you used to call me Go when we were babies and then it became Joe."

As I lay back down, several thoughts ran through my mind. Without acknowledgement, I pushed each one aside. I would not allow any one of them to ruin the moment. The sun beat down on me but I basked in perfect security, aware that for a while I would be without it, rootless. *Or would I?* I stared at the ring. *So many questions and not enough years to spend searching for answers. In the end, we come back to what was right before our eyes.*

There was little in my life I could not live without. Even my parents did not escape the indifference and detachment that lurked beneath my skin. Joe was the only exception. Without him I was nothing, I had nothing to identify myself with. He was my reason for being. He was my spiritual home on Earth and my life existed within his beating heart. I kissed him gently until he opened his eyes.

"What?"

"You're everything I've ever wanted."

My mother had been absolutely furious when I told her about Joe's proposal.

"You're too young to be thinking about marriage, Genevieve!" Her eyes had been huge and she stood with her hands on her hips, weight thrown forward. She towered above me but was not menacing in the way Vanessa could be. There was no nastiness in my mother's anger - just pure, unadulterated rage. I could tolerate that. Seeing an absence of any emotion on my face, she had changed tack. "You're pregnant, aren't you?"

"No, I'm not pregnant and we've been talking about this for a couple of years now."

"A couple of years? You're seventeen!"

"Yes, I know that."

"I want you to go to university."

"I know that too."

"Padraig, she's your daughter! You tell her!" She'd looked at Dad, utterly crushed and pleading with eyes that had somehow grown even larger than her angry ones.

"Look, Eloise, Joe is a sensible boy." Mum's eyes had achieved the impossible – they'd grown even bigger.

"You know all about this? My own husband! Traitor!"

"Joe asked for her hand a couple of weeks ago. I wanted to tell you but you had that conference in Birmingham and then I forgot…"

"How could you forget something like this?"

"Look, Eloise…"

Mum had guffawed and turned away from him. She began to slap her own forehead. *Why would she do that? Surely it's painful?*

"I said look!" Dad had bellowed. The blood rushed to his face, turning it pink. "She's not that much younger than we were when we got engaged. And she's a damn sight more sensible."

"No! She's seventeen! She's still a… a…"

"Mum, I couldn't be less of a baby if I tried." My tone had been so devoid of emotion that I barely recognised my own voice. It sounded as though I were inside a tin. Mum sat down and scraped her hair away from her face. For the first time I'd noticed that she had begun to grey at the temples. *When did that start to happen?* I thought. She looked up at me with sad eyes.

"Did you ask Marcus for his advice?"

I burst out laughing. It was the most ridiculous question and was the last thing I expected to hear. Michael Davis had come and stood next to me then, putting his hand on my shoulder and squeezing it to show his support. *You're going to stand by me. I understand. Thank you so very much.* He smiled and walked away.

Dad had sat down at the table opposite Mum and clasped his hands around hers. Suddenly I saw them as they must have been thirty years ago as a young couple, sitting, talking, contemplating their future together. It was an intimate moment and I decided to leave them alone. As I reached the door I turned around and tried to put Mum's mind at ease before I left.

"We're not getting married yet, you know. Probably in another five years. We're not stupid."

"See, Eloise," Dad chipped in, "they're sensible kids." He winked at me as I left.

"No, they're not!" I heard Mum cry just before she burst into tears. I'd closed the door very gently behind me and made my way towards Watling Avenue.

My grandmother had been ecstatic when I told her the news. She sat me down and we both gazed at my ring over a glass of port and chocolate cake.

"Just in case I'm not here for the wedding, I'd like to give you something now, darling."

"What do you mean in case you're not here?" I'd asked, a little anxious at my grandmother's death talk. She'd been saying things like that a lot lately. *What is she not telling me? She's fine and my gut is saying nothing either.*

"Darling, I'm ninety. Do you really think people live forever?"

"You're ninety?"

"Yes, my dear, almost one hundred. And I'm not holding on for a letter from the Queen, I can assure you."

"But you can't be."

"Why not?"

"I don't know. You just can't be. Does Dad know?"

"Of course he does. He's my son. And my youngest at fifty-three, so he shouldn't have gone senile yet." Grandma had left me to gather my thoughts, after scattering them far and wide with her bombshell. She returned a few minutes later holding a small velvet box. It was red in the creases but the rest of it had faded to white. I opened it. Inside was a pair of earrings, aquamarines set in silver.

"I wore them on my wedding day. Your great-grandfather gave them to me. Said they complemented my black hair beautifully. I want you to wear them when you marry. Something borrowed, something blue. I've already given my wedding band to Joe for safe keeping until the big day."

"You've seen Joe already?" I'd been astounded.

"Well, yes, darling. He wanted to ask my permission. Apparently, I'm your favourite person. Fancy that!" She winked at me like Dad often did and took a large sip of port.

"But Grandma, you seemed so genuinely surprised!"

"I was a very good actress, you know."

It was a cool, clear morning. The dew on the cobwebs turned them into silver filigree, draped over the bushes like an endless shawl. Canons Park was at its most beautiful in the early hours of the morning. I stood in the centre of it, arms outstretched, as if welcoming a silent embrace. I turned full circle, feasting my eyes on a panoramic view that would become etched in my photographic memory. I would take it with me everywhere. We were inseparable now. Tears rolled out of my smiling eyes as I made my way towards the stables. Today I'd come to bid farewell to Matthew.

He was inside, flinging fresh hay onto the floor and patting the horses as he passed them, personally greeting each one. Once again, I stood watching, drinking in another precious reminder of the life I was about to leave behind.

"Genevieve, I'm waiting for you to speak, so make yourself known. Don't stand there like an apparition."

"What's the point in saying something if you already know I'm here?"

"Don't talk back, young lady." He threw a piece of dung at me. I didn't move and it missed. *He's trying to be playful. I'll be troublesome for old time's sake.*

"You just told me to say something and then told me off for it. That was a bad shot by the way."

The next piece of dung hit me on the chin. Luckily it was bone dry and crumbled without doing any damage. It smelled horrendous. Matthew had his back to me but I saw his shoulders shake momentarily. When he turned to face me again his face was emotionless.

"Matthew, I've come to say goodbye."

"Aye."

I waited for him to continue. Often, particularly when he felt an emotion strongly, Matthew would become quiet so that he could choose his words carefully.

"I knew this time would come. You weren't going to remain a child forever."

"No." This time he waited for me.

"I'm going away. University, in France. Then I'll come back and marry Joe."

"I always thought you should get out for a while. You're clever and restless, Genevieve." I was astonished at his liberal attitude. Where was his characteristic old-fashioned chauvinism?

"You're not going to tell me off, Matthew?"

"Should I?"

"No."

"I'm a man of convention, aye," he said, very slowly, "but you're a sensible young woman now and I want more for you than endless work, keeping home and an unworthy marriage." He hesitated. I realised then that I'd become the child that Matthew had never had the opportunity to bring up, love and let go of. "Genevieve, as long as you remember where you came from, you have my blessing."

"Can I give you a hug?" I asked, stretching my arms out.

"No."

"Why not?"

"It's inappropriate behaviour in a lady your age."

"But you've just given me your blessing and..."

"It can be revoked, Genevieve."

"Oh, never mind."

I thanked Matthew by helping him muck out the stables. By the time I went home for breakfast, I was covered in horse poo and stank like a compost heap. Nobody noticed except Dad, who kept accusing me of farting.

Taking a deep breath, I pushed the door open and let it creak painfully until it hit the wall. It was a scene I had revisited often and I recalled the first time I had entered this bedroom. Years had passed but the room still felt like a black hole of time waiting to swallow me. This was not going to be my room for much longer. I entered silently and closed the door, to keep the rest of the world out.

"Evelyn," I called softly. "Evelyn Bingham, it's me, Genevieve. I'd like to talk to you, woman to woman."

The atmosphere stiffened and the air cooled significantly. I could not see her but I knew she was there.

"Evelyn, I know you can hear me," I continued. A book flew off the chest of drawers and landed on my foot, hurting me. I did not react visibly although I was cursing inside. "The problem is, Evelyn, I know what you did to John. I know what you did to Margaret and Michael. It's murder and I can't rest knowing that."

"You know nothing!" I heard her hiss next to my ear. Shocked by the suddenness of her reply, I tried to turn my head in its direction but couldn't. My neck was so cold it had started to hurt and there was an overpowering smell of something acrid. My breathing became shallower and I was struggling.

"You did… you used… arsenic… I know. I know." I croaked.

The air around me grew thicker until I could no longer draw any into my lungs. My eyesight began to blur. I began to panic and wondered if she was trying to kill me.

"Evelyn," I gasped, "one thing is for certain - I am not… not afraid of you… and will have you banished… by force if I have to. Please help yourself… by choosing not… not to remain stagnant anymore."

There was a bursting sensation in my throat and the constriction around it eased as suddenly as it had manifested.

Well done, Genevieve, you speak a truth that needed to be spoken, came a whispering on the breeze that the release had produced. I watched it as it wafted past, the dark grey turning to a brilliant blue as it ascended past my head. The air became warm again and I felt an intense rush of energy in my legs and abdomen that pushed me to stand up.

"It is now almost the twenty-first century and about time you moved on. Don't you want to move on?" I asked loudly.

I turned to find Evelyn standing beside me. The harsh look on her face had started to soften as her hand fell away from the crucifix that hung on her waist.

"What did you say?" she asked, apparently confused. "Twenty-first?"

As I watched the transformation in front of me I began to realise that Evelyn had had no idea that she'd kept herself captive in time. Her mask of severity and hatred began to fall away and behind it I could see her for what she truly was: cowardly, vulnerable and… human.

"Why did you do it?" I asked.

"And why not?" she countered bitterly. "I come from nothing, at my brother's charity only to have their happiness thrown in my face! I prayed to God my whole life for some of my own. Where was God then? And to be lumbered with that pathetic, sickly little boy. He couldn't even walk by himself without coughing. I hate them! I hate them all!"

She collapsed and began to weep into her hands. I noticed that they were dainty hands, with long fingers and smooth skin. She was probably only in her thirties, which shocked me to the core.

"You were illegitimate, weren't you, Evelyn?"

She stopped crying and looked up at me. The vulnerability in her eyes made me stagger backwards until I hit the wall. I closed my eyes to try and shield myself from it but it was too late. A spectrum of emotions ran through my heart, each one a memory of our journey together over the years. In that moment in time I was able to understand why Evelyn had chosen the way she did. I didn't have to choose to forgive her, it just happened.

"Michael was only trying to help you by bringing you here to get a better life," I heard myself say. "And John Graham was sick because he had tuberculosis, it wasn't his fault. He just grew weaker and weaker."

Evelyn nodded and got up. She didn't smile but her face had softened until its rightful youthfulness reappeared. The pale, rapidly diffusing energy around her told me she was ready to go. I watched as she faded and for a long time afterwards there was a tingling in the air that my hands seemed to absorb and enjoy feeling. It was the end of an era and I knew that by setting her free I had also freed myself of a burden I had unwittingly shouldered for a large part of my young life.

The time had come for me to set out into the world as a grown woman. John Graham no longer needed me to protect him and the realisation of Evelyn's truth meant that Michael and Margaret could now rest in peace too. We had all been set free. At least for the time being.

Lying was not a habit I practised often. I had very little respect for it at the best of times. However, it was something I had to fall back on, the day I left home. If there was something I hated more than lying, it was painful and protracted goodbyes.

Marcus had just bought a flat of his own near Baker Street and had taken the week off work to pack and evacuate. Mum had spent the last few days moping and pretending she was perfectly happy to let go of her son. Dad was at Marcus' flat looking at the plumbing and electrics. Joe and I played our respective parts in facilitating the move by staying out of the way and carrying things to the car when ordered to do so. I was surprised at how much junk Marcus had accumulated over the years and that it had all fitted in his bedroom. On the whole, his moving out was a quiet affair that caused little more than a ripple in everybody's lives except Mum's.

John Graham and I sat by the bay window, watching Dad and Marcus put the last of the belongings in the car. Before he got in, Marcus turned around and took one last look at the house. He gave me a gentle nod and got in.

"Don't know why he's acting like a rock star," I said. "He's only twenty minutes away on the Tube."

"What's a rock star?" asked John Graham.

"Oh, I don't think they'd been invented in your time. Closest example would be, um, Marie Lloyd." He still looked blank. "It's a person who's famous for being talented but most of them nowadays aren't. Look, it doesn't matter."

We sat in silence for a while. My heart felt as though it were being squeezed. I was going to miss John Graham more than I'd imagined I would. I hadn't told him I was leaving too; there hadn't been any opportunity to discuss it recently.

"You're leaving today, aren't you?" he asked.

"Tomorrow. How did you guess?"

"I saw you putting your books into boxes and you gave some of your clothes away to the girl who lives a few doors away."

"I'm so sorry I didn't tell you in person. There wasn't time to..."

"It's alright, Genevieve, I knew this day was coming so I looked for the signs."

"You're very perceptive, John Graham."

"I learned from you." We smiled at one another, sadly. John Graham's eyes were clear whereas mine had misted over.

"I'm not sure what kind of person I'll become, you know. Will you still be my friend when I get back, John Graham? You know you don't have to stay anymore."

I began to cry. I tried gulping back the pangs of separation that had already begun to surface in my throat but it was no use. I started to wail and buried my face in the nearest sofa cushion. John Graham came and sat behind me, pressing his face into my hair.

"Don't cry, Genevieve. I'll definitely be here when you return and we'll be friends forever. We all have to go through frightening and uncertain times but they make us stronger."

"True," I hiccupped between sobs. "When did you become so wise?"

That night I slept fitfully and did not stir until my alarm clock jolted me back to consciousness. I sat in bed for a while looking at the room that I'd shared with John Graham over time, where I'd spent my most formative years. It seemed lifeless that morning, perhaps in anticipation of lying vacant over the next few years. I smiled at the walls. Last night was very nearly spent in Joe's bedroom. It had taken a Herculean effort on his part to tear himself away from me long enough to say, "Please Gen, I really want to do things right. I want to wait until we have our own space, not under my parents' roof."

Curling my left hand into a fist, I rested it against my chest so that my engagement ring was next to my heart. I could not cry this morning. Strength and certainty had found me once more and I was looking forward to whatever was to happen. Quickly and quietly I showered and packed the last of my belongings. The sight of my rucksack and sports bag made me laugh out loud.

"Seventeen years on Earth and this is all I have?"

Downstairs Mum and Dad had finished their breakfast. I heard the clattering of plates against metal as Mum washed up, and the shutting of cabinet doors as Dad put the dried crockery away. I had told them I'd be leaving in the evening but I planned to leave while they were at church. *I hate goodbyes. They're so goddamn final.* Hearing the car pull away, I picked up my bags and slowly walked down the stairs, savouring the sound of every creaking floorboard. I hated the house but I knew I was going to miss it terribly.

"Where are you going, petite?"

Mum was standing by the dining room door, in jeans and her cleaning-up shirt, looking worried. For a moment I didn't speak, just looked back at her. She looked different today, vulnerable. I had never seen my mother looking vulnerable before, not even when Vanessa and Marcus had left. Her eyes were strangely soft, almost as though they were telling me they loved me because the rest of her could not.

"I'm going. Now," I said, as gently as possible.

"Why?"

"Because I hate goodbyes and fuss. Why aren't you in church? It's Sunday."

"Your father and Marcus are watching rugby. Can church compete with rugby?"

She had a point there. Sometimes I wondered why Mum had never tried to develop a sense of humour. She came up with some great one-liners. I picked my bags up again. Mum rushed towards me with her arms outstretched, hugging me tenderly for several minutes. Suddenly, she looked old and fragile, almost submissive, knowing there was nothing she could do to stop me leaving. One by one, each and every one of her children had left her and she had never allowed herself the time to process it all, creating extra work and invisible responsibility to avoid that. And yet my departure was different. As she held me, I felt more than just grief. There was the realisation that her youngest child was always going to be a stranger to her. I had reached adulthood now and there would be no more time or opportunity to share my childhood. It hurt her more than she had ever contemplated and I could feel her pain.

"Wait!" she said, drying her eyes with her sleeve and smudging mascara all over her face, "I'll give you money. You can't go without money, food and clothes. Wait here, I'll get my handbag and we can go to the cash point on the way. I'll drop you."

Without looking back at me she ran up the stairs and I took the opportunity to exit quietly. As usual, she would search frantically upstairs, cursing Dad for tidying haphazardly when all the time her handbag would be downstairs on the sofa, where Michael Davis now leaned as he smoked his pipe. I winked at him as I approached the front door, silently passing into the next phase of my life's journey.

Outside, the sun was waiting for me to emerge. It accompanied me on the short walk to the station. As I passed Canons, I turned to look at the droves of people, dead and alive, being absorbed into the church. I knew I'd be back one day. This place was in my blood. It had shaped me thus far and was now just entrusting my life to somewhere else for a while.

One day it would call me back to finish what destiny had begun.

To be continued…

If you have enjoyed this book...

Local Legend is committed to publishing the very best spiritual writing, both fiction and non-fiction. You might also enjoy:

A Single Petal
Oliver Eade (ISBN 978-1-907203-42-8)

Winner of the national Local Legend Spiritual Writing Competition, this page-turner is a novel of murder, politics and passion set in ancient China. Yet its themes of loyalty, commitment and deep love are every bit as relevant for us today as they were in past times. The author is an expert on Chinese culture and history, and his debut adult novel deserves to become a classic.

Indigo Awakes
Stephanie de Winter (ISBN 978-1-907203-44-2)

One woman's journey from a life of abuse and depression to finding her spiritual path and personal healing, guided by dreams and synchronicities. This stunning debut novel, written in simple language, does not only speak to women but teaches us all how to turn our lives around. A sequel is on the way too!

The Quirky Medium
Alison Wynne-Ryder (ISBN 978-1-907203-47-3)

Alison is the co-host of the TV show *Rescue Mediums*, in which she puts herself in real danger to free homes of lost and often malicious spirits. Yet she is a most reluctant medium, afraid of ghosts! This is her astonishing autobiography, telling how her amazing gifts developed and taking us 'back stage' of the television production.

5P1R1T R3V3L4T10N5
Nigel Peace (ISBN 978-1-907203-14-5)

With descriptions of more than a hundred proven prophetic dreams and many more everyday synchronicities, the author shows us that everyone can receive genuine spiritual guidance for our ordinary life challenges. World-renowned biologist Dr Rupert Sheldrake has endorsed this book as "...vivid and fascinating... pioneering research..." The author, a mathematician and philosopher, has lectured to the Society for Psychical Research, the College of Psychic Studies and elsewhere.

Further details and extracts of these and many
other beautiful titles may be seen at
www.local-legend.co.uk

Lightning Source UK Ltd.
Milton Keynes UK
UKHW020104160620
365054UK00022B/6149